THE AUSTRALIAN
Women's Weekly

CAKES
& Cupcakes

CONTENTS

....

show stoppers

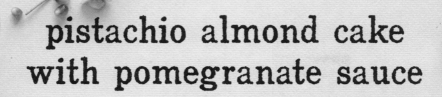

pistachio almond cake
with pomegranate sauce

PREP + COOK TIME 1½ HOURS (+ REFRIGERATION & COOLING) • SERVES 12

2 cups (560g) greek-style yoghurt

1 cup (160g) almond kernels

1 cup (140g) unsalted pistachios

4 eggs, separated

¾ cup (165g) caster (superfine) sugar

1 cup (120g) ground almonds

40g (1½ ounces) butter, melted

1 cup (160g) icing (confectioners') sugar

1 medium pomegranate (320g)

POMEGRANATE SAUCE

2 medium pomegranates (620g)

¼ cup (55g) caster (superfine) sugar

1 tablespoon cornflour (cornstarch)

1 Place yoghurt in a fine strainer lined with muslin or paper towel; place over jug or bowl. Cover; refrigerate overnight.

2 Preheat oven to 160°C/325°F. Grease a deep 25cm (10-inch) round cake pan; line base with baking paper.

3 Spread almonds, in a single layer, on oven tray; roast, uncovered, in oven, for 10 minutes, stirring frequently. Add pistachios; roast a further 2 minutes. Remove nuts from tray; cool. Process nuts until coarsely ground.

4 Beat egg whites and caster sugar in a small bowl with an electric mixer until sugar dissolves. Beat in egg yolks. Transfer mixture to a large bowl; stir in nuts, ground almonds and melted butter.

5 Spread mixture into pan. Bake cake for 45 minutes. Cool cake in pan.

6 Meanwhile, make pomegranate sauce.

7 Whisk drained yoghurt and sifted icing sugar in a medium bowl until soft peaks form.

8 Halve pomegranate; remove seeds. Serve cake with yoghurt mixture, seeds and pomegranate sauce.

pomegranate sauce Cut pomegranates in half, squeeze on citrus juicer. You need 1 cup juice. Combine sugar and cornflour in a small saucepan, gradually stir in juice. Cook, stirring, over high heat until mixture boils and thickens. Cool.

Test Kitchen
NOTES

Start this recipe the day
before required. Store the
cake in an airtight container
in fridge for up to two days.

Store cake in the refrigerator for up to two days. Bring to room temperature before serving.

layered banana butterscotch cake

PREP + COOK TIME 2 HOURS (+ COOLING & REFRIGERATION) • SERVES 12

You'll need 4 overripe large bananas for this recipe.

375g (12 ounces) butter, softened

2 cups (440g) caster (superfine) sugar

6 eggs

2 cups mashed overripe bananas

3 cups (450g) self-raising flour

½ cup (75g) plain (all-purpose) flour

3 cups (360g) pecan halves

BUTTERSCOTCH FROSTING

1½ cups (330g) firmly packed brown sugar

¾ cup (180ml) pouring cream

185g (6 ounces) butter

375g (12 ounces) cream cheese

BUTTERSCOTCH SAUCE

185g (6 ounces) butter, chopped

1 cup (220g) firmly packed brown sugar

1 cup (250ml) pouring cream

1 Preheat oven to 180°C/350°F. Grease two deep 20cm (8-inch) round cake pans; line bases with baking paper.

2 Make butterscotch frosting and butterscotch sauce.

3 Beat butter and sugar in a large bowl with an electric mixer until light and fluffy. Beat in eggs, one at a time. Stir in banana, then sifted flours. Divide mixture evenly between pans.

4 Bake cakes about 50 minutes. Stand cakes in pan for 5 minutes before turning, top-side up, onto wire racks to cool.

5 Place nuts, in a single layer, on oven tray; Roast, in oven, for 10 minutes or until browned lightly, stirring frequently. Remove from tray, cool; chop nuts coarsely.

6 Trim tops of cakes to make level. Split cakes in half (see page 113). Place one cake layer, cut-side up, on serving plate; spread with ¼ cup butterscotch sauce, then ½ cup butterscotch frosting.

7 Spread cut surface of next cake layer with another ¼ cup butterscotch sauce; place, sauce-side down, on top of first layer. Spread top of cake with another ¼ cup sauce, then ½ cup frosting.

8 Repeat layering with remaining cake, finishing with frosting. Spread remaining frosting over side of cake. Press nuts onto side of cake. Refrigerate cake 2 hours or until firm.

9 Serve cake drizzled with remaining sauce.

butterscotch frosting Stir sugar, cream and half the butter in a small saucepan over medium heat until smooth. Bring to the boil, stirring constantly. Reduce heat; simmer, uncovered, 5 minutes. Transfer mixture to a large heatproof bowl; refrigerate until cold. Beat remaining butter with cream cheese in a medium bowl with an electric mixer until combined. Gradually beat in cold butterscotch mixture. Cover; refrigerate about 1½ hours or until spreadable.

butterscotch sauce Place ingredients in a medium saucepan; cook, stirring, until smooth. Bring to the boil. Reduce heat; simmer, uncovered, for 3 minutes. Transfer to a medium heatproof bowl. Cover; place in refrigerator until cold.

lemon cake with lemon mascarpone frosting

PREP + COOK TIME 1½ HOURS (+ COOLING) • SERVES 8

125g (4 ounces) butter, softened

2 teaspoons finely grated lemon rind

1¼ cups (275g) caster (superfine) sugar

3 eggs

1½ cups (225g) self-raising flour

½ cup (125ml) milk

¼ cup (60ml) lemon juice

lemon yellow food colouring

6 white sugar coated almonds, smashed

6 yellow sugar coated almonds, smashed

LEMON MASCARPONE FROSTING

1 cup (250ml) thickened (heavy) cream

½ cup (80g) icing (confectioners') sugar

2 teaspoons finely grated lemon rind

⅔ cup (170g) mascarpone cheese

SYRUPY LEMON SLICES

¼ cup (55g) caster (superfine) sugar

2 tablespoons lemon juice

1 tablespoon honey

2 tablespoons water

1 medium lemon (140g), sliced thinly

1 Preheat oven to 180°C/350°F. Grease a deep 20cm (8-inch) round cake pan; line base with baking paper.

2 Make lemon mascarpone frosting; refrigerate, covered, until required.

3 Beat butter, rind and sugar in a small bowl with an electric mixer until light and fluffy. Beat in eggs, one at a time (mixture might separate at this stage, but will come together later); transfer mixture to a large bowl. Stir in sifted flour, milk and juice, in two batches; tint cake with a few drops of yellow colouring. Pour mixture into pan.

4 Bake cake about 50 minutes. Stand cake in pan for 5 minutes before turning, top-side up, onto a wire rack to cool.

5 Meanwhile, make syrupy lemon slices.

6 Split cold cake into three layers (see page 113), place one layer onto a serving plate, cut-side up; spread with one-third of the frosting. Repeat layering, finishing with frosting. Decorate cake with cooled lemon slices; sprinkle over crushed nuts and drizzle with reserved syrup.

lemon mascarpone frosting Beat cream, sifted icing sugar and rind in a small bowl with an electric mixer until soft peaks form; fold in mascarpone.

syrupy lemon slices Stir sugar, juice, honey and the water in a small saucepan over medium heat, without boiling, until sugar dissolves. Bring to the boil, then reduce heat to a simmer (do not stir). Add lemon slices, three at a time. Cook, without stirring, for 2 minutes or until lemon slices start to soften. Remove slices, transfer to a plate to cool. Repeat with remaining lemon slices. Reserve syrup.

This cake will keep in an airtight container in the fridge for up to three days.

pistachio and rosewater layer cake

200g (6½ ounces) roasted unsalted pistachios

250g (8 ounces) butter, softened

1½ cups (330g) caster (superfine) sugar

2 teaspoons finely grated lemon rind

4 eggs

1 cup (150g) plain (all-purpose) flour

½ cup (75g) self-raising flour

¾ cup (200g) greek-style yoghurt

turkish delight, chopped coarsely, optional, to decorate

ROSEWATER BUTTER CREAM

250g (8 ounces) butter, softened

2 teaspoons rosewater

3 cups (480g) icing (confectioners') sugar

1 tablespoon milk, approximately

1 Preheat oven to 170°C/340°F. Grease a deep 22cm (9-inch) round cake pan; line base and side with baking paper.

2 Blend or process 1 cup of the nuts until finely ground. Coarsely chop remaining nuts.

3 Beat butter, sugar and rind in a medium bowl with an electric mixer until light and fluffy. Beat in eggs, one at a time. Stir in sifted flours, yoghurt and ground nuts. Spread mixture into pan.

4 Bake cake about 1¼ hours. Stand cake in pan for 5 minutes before turning, top-side up, onto a wire rack to cool.

5 Make rosewater butter cream.

6 Split cooled cake in half (see page 113). Place bottom layer, cut-side up, onto a serving plate; spread with one-third of the butter cream, top with remaining cake layer. Spread remaining butter cream all over cake; sprinkle chopped nuts on top of cake. Decorate with turkish delight, if you like.

rosewater butter cream Beat butter and rosewater in a medium bowl with an electric mixer until as white as possible. Gradually beat in sifted icing sugar until smooth. Add enough of the milk to make the butter cream a spreadable consistency.

choc-caramel brownie ice-cream sandwich

300g (9½ ounces) dark (semi-sweet) chocolate

185g (6 ounces) butter, chopped

¼ cup (25g) dutch-processed cocoa powder

1 cup (220g) firmly packed brown sugar

¾ cup (165g) caster (superfine) sugar

2 teaspoons vanilla extract

4 eggs

1½ cups (225g) plain (all-purpose) flour

2 cups (500ml) caramel swirl ice-cream

CHOCOLATE GANACHE

300ml pouring cream

200g (6½ ounces) dark (semi-sweet) chocolate

ALMOND TOFFEE

100g (3 ounces) blanched almonds

1 cup (220g) caster (superfine) sugar

½ cup (125ml) water

1 Preheat oven to 160°C/325°F. Grease two 20cm (8-inch) square cake pans; line with baking paper, extending paper 5cm (2 inches) over sides.

2 Break chocolate into a large heatproof bowl; add butter. Place over a large saucepan of simmering water; stir until smooth. Remove from heat; whisk in sifted cocoa, sugars and extract until smooth. Stir in eggs and sifted flour.

3 Spread mixture evenly into pans. Bake about 35 minutes; cool brownies in pans. Enclose brownies in plastic wrap, freeze until ready to assemble.

4 Soften ice-cream slightly. Line a cleaned 20cm (8-inch) square pan with plastic wrap. Evenly spread ice-cream into pan, smoothing top; freeze.

5 Cut each brownie into 16 x 5cm (2-inch) slices. Turn ice-cream onto a board; cut into 16 x 5cm slices. Sandwich ice-cream between brownie slices.

6 Make chocolate ganache and almond toffee.

7 Top brownie sandwich with ganache and toffee.

chocolate ganache Bring cream to the boil in a small saucepan; remove from heat. Break chocolate into cream; stir until smooth. Transfer mixture to a small bowl. Refrigerate until firm. Beat ganache with an electric mixer until spreadable.

almond toffee Stir nuts in a large heavy-based frying pan until golden; remove from pan to baking-paper-lined oven tray to cool. Combine sugar and the water in a small saucepan, stir over high heat, without boiling, until sugar is dissolved. Bring to the boil; boil, without stirring, for 10 minutes or until mixture turns a golden colour. Remove from heat, allow bubbles to subside. Pour toffee evenly over nuts; leave to set at room temperature. Break roughly into pieces.

Test Kitchen NOTES

Use a large, sharp hot dry kitchen knife to cut the brownie sandwich into squares. If you are not going to serve it all, it's best to only cut what you need as the cut brownie will dry out in the freezer. Cover the cut surfaces with plastic wrap and freeze before it melts.

strawberries and cream white chocolate roulade

5 eggs, separated

⅔ cup (150g) caster (superfine) sugar

1½ tablespoons hot water

80g (2½ ounces) white chocolate, grated finely

⅔ cup (100g) self-raising flour

¼ cup (55g) caster (superfine) sugar, extra

375g (12 ounces) strawberries, sliced thinly

2 tablespoons icing (confectioners') sugar

½ teaspoon sumac

250g (8 ounces) mascarpone cheese

½ cup (125ml) thickened (heavy) cream

30g (1 ounce) store-bought meringue nests, crushed coarsely

1 Preheat oven to 200°C/400°F. Grease a 26cm x 32cm (10½-inch x 12¾-inch) swiss roll pan; line base and long sides with baking paper, extending the paper 5cm (2 inches) over sides.

2 Beat egg yolks and caster sugar in a medium bowl with an electric mixer for 5 minutes or until very thick and pale. Pour the hot water down the inside of the bowl, add chocolate; gently fold in sifted flour until just combined. Transfer to a medium bowl.

3 Beat egg whites in a medium bowl with an electric mixer until soft peaks form. Fold egg whites into chocolate mixture, in two batches, until just combined. Spread mixture into pan.

4 Bake cake for 12 minutes or until golden and sponge springs back when pressed lightly with a finger.

5 Meanwhile, place a piece of baking paper, cut just larger than the pan, on a work surface; sprinkle evenly with extra sugar. Turn hot sponge onto sugar-covered-paper, peel away lining paper (see page 112); trim crisped edges with a sharp knife. Working quickly, and using paper as a guide, roll sponge up from one long side. Cool for 5 minutes. Unroll sponge, remove paper; reroll, cover with a clean tea towel. Cool.

6 Meanwhile, combine strawberries, sifted icing sugar and half the sumac in a medium bowl. Cover; refrigerate for 30 minutes.

7 Beat mascarpone and cream in a small bowl with an electric mixer until almost firm peaks form.

8 Unroll cooled sponge; spread with two-thirds of the cream mixture, leaving a 2.5cm (1-inch) border on all sides. Top with half the crushed meringue and half the strawberry mixture. Reroll sponge to enclose filling.

9 Serve roulade topped with remaining cream, meringue and strawberry mixture; sprinkle with remaining sumac.

raspberry layered cake

185g (6 ounces) white eating chocolate, chopped coarsely

90g (3 ounces) unsalted butter, chopped coarsely

1 cup (250ml) buttermilk

1¼ cups (275g) caster (superfine) sugar

3 eggs

1 teaspoon vanilla extract

1 cup (150g) plain (all-purpose) flour

½ cup (75g) self-raising flour

½ teaspoon bicarbonate of soda (baking soda)

pink food colouring

¼ cup (80g) raspberry jam, warmed, strained, cooled

1 punnet (125g) fresh raspberries

FLUFFY MOCK CREAM FROSTING

⅓ cup (80ml) milk

⅔ cup (160ml) water

2 cups (440g) caster (superfine) sugar

2 teaspoons gelatine

⅓ cup (80ml) water, extra

500g (1 pound) unsalted butter, softened

2 teaspoons vanilla extract

1 Preheat oven to 150°C/300°F. Grease two 17cm (6¾-inch) round cake pans; line bases and sides with baking paper, extending the paper 5cm (2 inches) above sides.

2 Stir chocolate, butter and buttermilk in a medium saucepan over low heat until smooth. Transfer to a large bowl; cool 10 minutes.

3 Whisk sugar, eggs and extract into chocolate mixture. Whisk in sifted dry ingredients until mixture is smooth and glossy; tint light pink with a few drops of food colouring. Divide mixture evenly into pans.

4 Bake cakes for 1 hour. Stand cakes in pans for 5 minutes before turning, top-side up, onto wire racks to cool.

5 Make fluffy mock cream frosting.

6 Split cold cakes in half; brush layers with jam, then sandwich with mock cream. Spread cake all over with remaining frosting. Top with berries.

fluffy mock cream frosting Stir milk, the water and sugar in a medium saucepan over heat, without boiling, until sugar dissolves. Sprinkle gelatine over the extra water in a cup, add to pan; stir syrup until gelatine is dissolved. Cool to room temperature. Beat butter and extract in a medium bowl with an electric mixer until as white as possible. With motor operating, gradually pour in cold syrup in a thin, steady stream; beat until light and fluffy. (The mixture will thicken on standing.)

orange blossom and raspberry angel food cake

PREP + COOK TIME 50 MINUTES (+ COOLING) • SERVES 12

125g (4 ounces) frozen raspberries, thawed

½ cup (75g) plain (all-purpose) flour

½ cup (75g) wheaten cornflour (cornstarch)

1¼ cups (275g) caster (superfine) sugar

12 egg whites

1 teaspoon cream of tartar

2 teaspoons orange blossom water

¼ cup organic edible flowers

ORANGE BLOSSOM ICING

2 cups (320g) icing (confectioners') sugar

¼ teaspoon orange blossom water

¼ cup (60ml) strained lemon juice

1 Adjust oven shelf to lowest position. Preheat oven to 180°C/350°F.

2 Push raspberries through a fine sieve into a small bowl; discard seeds. Sift flours and ¼ cup of the sugar together five times.

3 Beat egg whites in a large bowl with an electric mixer until soft peaks form (see page 113); beat in cream of tartar. Gradually add remaining sugar, beating until sugar dissolves and mixture is very thick and glossy. Whisk in orange blossom water. Sift one-third of the flour mixture over meringue; gently fold through using a balloon whisk. Repeat with remaining flour mixture, in batches.

4 Transfer one-third of the cake mixture to a medium bowl; fold in raspberry puree. Carefully fold raspberry mixture into remaining cake mixture, swirling to create a marbled effect. Spoon mixture into an ungreased 25cm (10-inch) angel food cake pan with a removable base; smooth surface.

5 Bake cake for 30 minutes or until cake springs back when pressed lightly with a finger.

6 Place a piece of baking paper, just larger than the pan, on a work surface. Immediately turn hot pan upside-down on the paper; leave to cool completely in this position. The cake will drop when cold; if not, you may need to run a spatula around the cake to release it.

7 Make orange blossom icing. Drizzle cooled cake with icing; decorate with flowers.

orange blossom icing Sift icing sugar into a small bowl; stir in orange blossom water and enough of the juice to form an icing the consistency of honey.

blackberry lemon cake with blackberry fool

125g (4 ounces) butter, softened

¾ cup (165g) caster (superfine) sugar

1 tablespoon finely grated lemon rind

2 eggs

1 cup (150g) self-raising flour

½ cup (60g) ground almonds

125g (4 ounces) sour cream

150g (4½ ounces) frozen blackberries

2 tablespoons lemon juice

2 tablespoons water

⅓ cup (75g) caster (superfine) sugar, extra

1 tablespoon icing (confectioners') sugar

1 cup (250ml) thickened (heavy) cream

1 Preheat oven to 170°C/340°F. Grease a 9cm x 22cm x 9.5cm (3¾-inch x 9-inch x 4-inch) loaf pan; line base and long sides with baking paper, extending paper 5cm (2 inches) over sides.

2 Beat butter, caster sugar and rind in a large bowl with an electric mixer until pale and fluffy. Beat in eggs, one at a time, until combined. Fold in sifted flour, then ground almonds and sour cream.

3 Spoon half the mixture into pan; top with ¼ cup of the blackberries, pressing lightly into the mixture. Top with remaining cake mixture and another ¼ cup of the blackberries; smooth surface. Tap pan on a work surface to settle mixture.

4 Bake cake for 1¼ hours or until a skewer inserted into the centre comes out clean. Stand cake in pan for 10 minutes.

5 Meanwhile, stir juice, the water and extra caster sugar in a small saucepan over medium heat until sugar dissolves. Bring to the boil. Reduce heat; simmer for 2 minutes. Cool for 5 minutes.

6 Pour hot syrup over cake in pan. Stand for 20 minutes before transferring to a wire rack to cool completely.

7 Combine remaining berries and any juices with sifted icing sugar in a small bowl; set aside until berries thaw completely. Crush lightly with a fork.

8 Beat cream in a large bowl with an electric mixer until soft peaks form.

9 Spoon cream on top of cake; drizzle with remaining berry mixture swirling lightly through cream.

Test Kitchen NOTES

This cake is best made on the day of serving. We used a loaf pan with a capacity of 1.5 litres (6 cups). Adding frozen berries to the cake mixture stops the colour from running into the batter.

passionfruit meringue cake

125g (4 ounces) butter

1 teaspoon vanilla extract

1¾ cups (385g) caster (superfine) sugar

2 eggs

¾ cup (110g) self-raising flour

2 tablespoons plain (all-purpose) flour

⅓ cup (80ml) milk

4 egg whites

½ teaspoon cream of tartar

1 teaspoon caster (superfine) sugar, extra

300ml thickened (heavy) cream, extra

1 tablespoon icing (confectioners') sugar, sifted

2 starfruit, sliced thinly

PASSIONFRUIT SAUCE

1 tablespoon caster (superfine') sugar

1 teaspoon cornflour (cornstarch)

⅓ cup passionfruit pulp

⅓ cup water

PASSIONFRUIT CREAM

300ml thickened (heavy) cream

250g (8 ounces) mascarpone cheese

2 tablespoons passionfruit pulp

2 tablespoons icing (confectioners') sugar

1 Preheat oven to 180°C/350°F. Grease two closed 22cm (9-inch) round springform pans; line base and side of pans with baking paper.

2 Beat butter, extract and ¾ cup of the sugar in a small bowl with an electric mixer until light and fluffy. Beat in eggs, one at a time. Transfer mixture to a large bowl; fold in combined sifted flours and milk, in two batches. Spread mixture evenly into pans.

3 Beat egg whites and cream of tartar in a small bowl with an electric mixer until soft peaks form. Gradually add remaining sugar, beating until sugar is dissolved between additions and mixture becomes thick and glossy. Spread meringue over cake mixture in pans. In one pan, smooth the meringue flat; in the other pan, use the back of a spoon to peak the meringue, then sprinkle with extra sugar.

4 Bake cakes for 30 minutes or until cooked when tested. Cool in pans.

5 Make passionfruit sauce. Make passionfruit cream.

6 Whip extra cream with the icing sugar in a medium bowl until soft peaks form.

7 Place the flat meringue-topped cake on a platter; spread with passionfruit cream. Place other cake, meringue side-up, on top. Dollop with whipped cream, top with star fruit and drizzle with passionfruit sauce.

passionfruit sauce Combine sugar and cornflour in a small saucepan, gradually stir in passionfruit pulp and water. Cook, stirring, over high heat until mixture boils and thickens. Cool.

passionfruit cream Beat cream in a small bowl with an electric mixer until soft peaks form. Combine mascarpone, passionfruit pulp and sifted icing sugar in a medium bowl; fold in whipped cream.

tips Invert the springform pan bases before closing so that they sit flat – this makes it easier to remove the cake from the bases. You will need 3 passionfruit for this recipe. The cakes can be made a day ahead. Assemble cake several hours before serving.

4 ways to decorate
CUPCAKES WITH CHOCOLATE

CHOCOLATE DRIZZLE

Half-fill the piping bag with white chocolate ganache. Pipe swirls of ganache on top of each chocolate cupcake. Melt a small block of dark chocolate (see page 112). Half-fill a disposable piping bag or ziptop bag with melted chocolate; cut a small opening in the end of the bag and drizzle chocolate over cupcake.

CHOCOLATE DIPPED

Half-fill the piping bag with white chocolate ganache. Pipe swirls of ganache on top of each chocolate cupcake. Place cakes in the freezer for 5 minutes or until icing is cold. Meanwhile, pour a bottle of Ice Magic into a small deep bowl. Dip cakes into chocolate to coat ganache; stand cupcakes until set.

CHOCOLATE SHAVINGS

Half-fill the piping bag with white chocolate ganache. Pipe swirls of ganache on top of each chocolate cupcake. Drag a vegetable peeler down the side of a small chocolate block to make little shavings and curls. Sprinkle cupcake with chocolate.

COCOA-DUSTED

Half-fill the piping bag with white chocolate ganache. Pipe swirls of ganache on top of each chocolate cupcake. Dust one half of each cupcake with some sifted cocoa.

chocolate, apricot and hazelnut cake

1⅔ cups (250g) dried apricots, chopped finely

½ cup (125ml) water

250g (8 ounces) butter, softened

2 cups (440g) firmly packed brown sugar

6 eggs

1 cup (150g) plain (all-purpose) flour

½ cup (75g) self-raising flour

¼ cup (25g) cocoa powder

1 cup (110g) ground hazelnuts

⅔ cup (160ml) buttermilk

CHOCOLATE BUTTERMILK CREAM

650g (1¼ pounds) milk chocolate, chopped

¾ cup (180ml) buttermilk

2¼ cups (360g) icing (confectioners') sugar

180g (5½ ounces) butter, softened

1 Combine apricots and the water in a small saucepan; bring to the boil. Reduce heat; simmer, covered, stirring occasionally, for 10 minutes or until apricot is soft. Cool.

2 Preheat oven to 160°C/325°F. Grease a deep 22cm (8-inch) round cake pan; line base with baking paper.

3 Beat butter and sugar in a small bowl with an electric mixer until light and fluffy. Beat in eggs, one at a time. Transfer mixture to a large bowl; stir in apricot mixture, sifted flours and cocoa, ground hazelnuts and buttermilk, in two batches. Spread mixture into pan.

4 Bake cake for 1¾ hours or until cooked when tested. Stand cake in pan for 10 minutes before turning, top-side up, onto a wire rack to cool.

5 Make chocolate buttermilk cream.

6 Split cold cake into three layers; sandwich layers with two-thirds of the buttermilk cream. Spread top of cake with remaining buttermilk cream. Top with chopped hazelnuts, if you like.

chocolate buttermilk cream Stir chocolate and buttermilk in a small heatproof bowl over a small saucepan of simmering water until smooth; stir in sifted icing sugar. Transfer mixture to the large bowl of an electric mixer. Beat on medium speed, gradually adding the butter, until mixture is smooth, thick and of a paler colour. Refrigerate, stirring occasionally, for 30 minutes or until mixture is spreadable.

Cake can be made a day ahead; cover, refrigerate. Bring to room temperature before serving.

We used Frangelico in this recipe, but you can use your favourite hazelnut liqueur.

raspberry hazelnut cake

PREP + COOK TIME 2 HOURS (+ COOLING TIME) • SERVES 12

250g (8 ounces) butter, softened

2 cups (440g) caster (superfine) sugar

6 eggs

1 cup (150g) plain (all-purpose) flour

½ cup (75g) self-raising flour

1 cup (110g) ground hazelnuts

⅔ cup (160g) sour cream

300g (9½ ounces) fresh or frozen raspberries

¼ cup whole hazelnuts, chopped coarsely

fresh or frozen raspberries, extra, to decorate

MASCARPONE CREAM

250g (8 ounces) mascarpone cheese

¼ cup (40g) icing (confectioners') sugar

2 tablespoons hazelnut liqueur

½ cup (120g) sour cream

½ cup (75g) roasted hazelnuts, chopped finely

1 Preheat oven to 180°C/350°F. Grease a deep 22cm (9-inch) round cake pan; line base and side with baking paper.

2 Beat butter and sugar in a medium bowl with an electric mixer until light and fluffy; add eggs, one at a time, beating until just combined between additions. (Mixture will curdle at this stage, but will come together later.)

3 Transfer mixture to a large bowl; using a wooden spoon, stir in sifted flours, ground hazelnuts, sour cream and raspberries. Spread mixture into pan.

4 Bake cake about 1½ hours. Stand cake in pan for 10 minutes before turning, top-side up, onto a wire rack to cool.

5 Make mascarpone cream; spread all over cake. Top with extra raspberries; sprinkle with chopped nuts. Dust with sifted icing sugar before serving, if you like.

mascarpone cream Combine mascarpone, sifted icing sugar, liqueur and sour cream in a medium bowl. Using a wooden spoon, stir until smooth; stir in nuts.

tips If using frozen raspberries, don't thaw them: frozen berries are less likely to 'bleed' into the cake mixture. Any berry of a similar size to raspberries can be used in this cake.
Any nut, such as almonds, pecans or walnuts, can be substituted for the ground hazelnuts; blend or process whole roasted nuts until fine. Choose a liqueur to complement the flavour of the nuts. Try amaretto with blueberries, almond meal and roasted chopped almond kernels.
The unfrosted cake will keep for up to 3 days in an airtight container at a cool room temperature. Cake can be frosted the day before required and stored in the refrigerator. Unfrosted cake can be frozen for up to 3 months.

lemon and earl grey chiffon syrup cake

PREP + COOK TIME 1½ HOURS (+ COOLING) • SERVES 12

2 cups (300g) self-raising flour

2 teaspoons french earl grey tea leaves

1½ cups (330g) caster (superfine) sugar

7 eggs, separated

¾ cup (180ml) strained lemon juice

½ cup (125ml) extra virgin olive oil

1 tablespoon finely grated lemon rind

½ teaspoon cream of tartar

600ml thickened (heavy) cream

2 tablespoons organic borage flowers (optional)

EARL GREY TEA SYRUP

1 tablespoon french earl grey tea leaves

1 cup (250ml) boiling water

1 cup (220g) caster (superfine) sugar

1 Adjust oven shelf to lowest position, place an oven tray on the shelf. Preheat oven to 180°C/350°F.

2 Triple-sift flour into a medium bowl.

3 Process tea leaves and ¾ cup of the sugar until leaves are finely chopped. Transfer mixture to a small bowl of an electric mixer, add egg yolks; beat for 5 minutes or until thick and pale. Gradually add juice, oil and half the rind, beating until well combined. Transfer mixture to a large bowl; sift flour over mixture, then fold gently with a whisk until just incorporated.

4 Beat egg whites in a large bowl with an electric mixer until soft peaks form (see page 113). Add cream of tartar, then gradually add remaining sugar, beating until mixture is thick and glossy. Fold egg white mixture into yolk mixture, in two batches, until just combined. Spoon mixture into an ungreased 25cm (10-inch) angel food cake pan with a removable base; gently smooth surface.

5 Place cake pan on the preheated oven tray; bake for 50 minutes or until cake springs back when pressed lightly with a finger. Place a piece of baking paper, just larger than the pan, on a work surface. Immediately turn hot pan upside-down onto the paper; leave to cool completely in this position. The cake will drop when cold; if not, you may need to run a spatula around the cake to release it.

6 Meanwhile, make earl grey tea syrup.

7 Beat cream in a small bowl with an electric mixer until soft peaks form; fold in remaining rind.

8 Using a serrated knife, split cake in half. Place the base layer on a cake plate; spread with a little more than half the cream. Top with remaining cake layer, then the cream. Decorate with flowers; drizzle with syrup.

earl grey tea syrup Combine tea leaves and the boiling water in a small saucepan; stand for 10 minutes. Add sugar; stir over low heat until sugar dissolves. Bring to the boil. Boil for 5 minutes or until syrup is reduced slightly. Cool, then strain.

cupcakes

earl grey cupcakes with honey meringue

PREP + COOK TIME 1 HOUR (+ COOLING) • MAKES 12

You need 12 (⅓-cup/80ml) ovenproof tea cups.

¼ cup (60ml) milk

3 earl grey tea bags

125g (4 ounces) butter, softened

1 teaspoon vanilla extract

¾ cup (165g) caster (superfine) sugar

3 eggs

1½ cups (225g) self-raising flour

HONEY MARSHMALLOW FROSTING

4 egg whites, beaten lightly

½ teaspoon cream of tartar

¾ cup (265g) honey

1 Preheat oven to 180°C/350°F. Place 12 greased ovenproof tea cups on two oven trays.

2 Heat milk in a small saucepan over high heat until simmering. Remove from heat. Add tea bags; stand for 10 minutes. Squeeze liquid from tea bags; discard bags.

3 Beat butter, extract, sugar, eggs, sifted flour and the infused milk in a small bowl with an electric mixer, on low speed, until ingredients are combined. Increase speed to medium; beat until mixture has changed to a paler colour. Divide mixture into cups. Bake about 20 minutes; cool cakes.

4 Make honey marshmallow frosting.

5 Working quickly dollop cold cakes with honey marshmallow frosting.

honey marshmallow frosting Place ingredients in a large heatproof bowl over a saucepan of simmering water; whisk with an electric mixer for 5 minutes or until mixture is thickened and sugar is dissolved. Remove from heat. Whisk for 5 minutes or until cooled to room temperature.

Test Kitchen
NOTES

If the frosting gets a little
soft, re-beat over a saucepan
of simmering water until
thickened. If you don't have
12 small ovenproof tea cups,
make the cupcakes in a 12-hole
⅓-cup (80ml) muffin pan lined
with paper cases.

Test Kitchen
NOTES

You can use thawed frozen
raspberries if you like, the
batter may be a bit thicker
if the berries are still cold.
Uniced cupcakes can be made
a day ahead or frozen for up
to 3 months. We placed the
cakes into decorative cupcake
wrappers to serve – do this
before decorating the cakes.

vanilla, white chocolate and raspberry cupcakes

PREP + COOK TIME 1½ HOURS (+ COOLING & REFRIGERATION) • MAKES 12

You need a sugar (candy) thermometer and a large piping bag fitted with a 1cm (½-inch) piping tube for this recipe.

½ cup (75g) fresh raspberries

1 vanilla bean, halved lengthways

125g (4 ounces) butter, softened

¾ cup (165g) caster (superfine) sugar

2 eggs

1½ cups (225g) self-raising flour

½ cup (125ml) milk

12 fresh raspberries, extra

FLUFFY FROSTING

1 cup (220g) caster (superfine) sugar

⅓ cup (80ml) water

3 egg whites

¼ cup (60g) pureed raspberries

1 Preheat oven to 180°C/350°F. Line a 12-hole (⅓-cup/80ml) muffin pan with paper cases.

2 Blend or process raspberries until smooth.

3 Scrape vanilla seeds from pod. Beat butter, sugar and vanilla seeds in a small bowl with an electric mixer until light and fluffy. Add eggs, one at a time; beating until just combined.

4 Transfer mixture to a large bowl. Stir in sifted flour and milk, in two batches. Lightly fold and swirl raspberry puree through mixture. Drop ¼-cups of mixture into paper cases.

5 Bake about 25 minutes. Stand cupcakes in pans for 5 minutes before turning top-side up, onto wire racks to cool.

6 Meanwhile, make fluffy frosting. Pipe the frosting onto the cakes; top with extra raspberries.

fluffy frosting Stir sugar and the water in a small saucepan over high heat, without boiling, until sugar is dissolved. Boil, uncovered, without stirring, for 5 minutes or until syrup reaches 114°C/240°F on a sugar thermometer. Remove from heat, allow the bubbles to subside. Begin to beat the egg whites in a small bowl with an electric mixer on a medium speed towards the end of the syrup's cooking time. Keep beating the egg whites while the sugar syrup reaches the correct temperature or the egg whites will deflate. With the mixer on medium speed, slowly pour in the hot syrup in a thin, steady stream; if the syrup is added too quickly, the frosting won't thicken. Once all the syrup is added, continue beating on medium to high speed for 10 minutes or until the mixture is thick and stands in stiff peaks; the frosting should be barely warm at this stage. Swirl pureed berries through frosting. Use frosting immediately.

margarita cupcakes

You need a large piping bag fitted with a 2cm (½-inch) plain tube for this recipe

180g (5½ ounces) butter, softened

1 teaspoon vanilla bean extract

1 tablespoon finely grated lime rind

1 cup (220g) caster (superfine) sugar

4 eggs

2 cups (300g) self-raising flour

2 tablespoons milk

⅓ cup (80ml) lime juice

2 tablespoons thinly sliced lime rind

1 teaspoon sea salt flakes

TEQUILA BUTTER CREAM

185g (6 ounces) unsalted butter, softened

2¼ cups (360g) icing (confectioners') sugar

¼ cup (60ml) tequila

1 Preheat oven to 180°C/350°F. Line a 12-hole (⅓-cup/80ml) muffin pan with paper cases.

2 Beat butter, extract, rind, sugar, eggs, sifted flour, milk and juice in a small bowl with an electric mixer on low speed until ingredients are combined. Increase speed to medium; beat until mixture has changed to a paler colour. Drop ¼ cups of mixture into paper cases.

3 Bake about 25 minutes. Stand cakes in pan for 5 minutes before turning, top-side up, onto a wire rack to cool.

4 Make tequila butter cream; spoon into piping bag; pipe large swirls on each cake. Sprinkle with lime and salt flakes.

tequila butter cream Beat butter in a small bowl with an electric mixer until as white as possible. Gradually beat in half the sifted icing sugar, tequila, then remaining icing sugar.

red wine and blueberry cupcakes

PREP + COOK TIME 1½ HOURS (+ REFRIGERATION & COOLING) • MAKES 12

125g (4 ounces) butter, softened

1 teaspoon vanilla extract

¾ cup (165g) firmly packed brown sugar

2 eggs

1¼ cups (185g) self-raising flour

¼ cup (25g) cocoa powder

1 cup (150g) fresh or frozen blueberries

250g (8-ounce) tub mascarpone cheese

1 tablespoon milk

1 tablespoon icing (confectioners') sugar

BLUEBERRY COMPOTE

1 cup (150g) fresh or frozen blueberries

2 tablespoons caster (superfine) sugar

1 cup (250ml) dry red wine

1 Make blueberry compote.

2 Preheat oven to 180°C/350°F. Line a 12-hole (⅓-cup/80ml) muffin pan with paper cases.

3 Beat butter, extract, brown sugar, eggs, sifted flour, cocoa and reserved wine mixture in a small bowl with an electric mixer on low speed until ingredients are combined. Increase speed to medium; beat until mixture has changed to a paler colour. Fold in blueberries. Divide mixture into paper cases.

4 Bake about 20 minutes. Stand cakes in pan for 5 minutes before turning, top-side up, onto a wire rack to cool.

5 Place mascarpone, milk and sifted icing sugar in a small bowl; stir to combine.

6 Remove and discard paper cases from cold cupcakes (see Test Kitchen notes). Place cupcakes in wine glasses. Top with dollops of mascarpone mixture, blueberries and syrup.

blueberry compote Place ingredients in a small bowl. Cover; refrigerate 2 hours. Drain blueberry mixture over a small saucepan; reserve blueberries. Heat wine mixture over low heat for 2 minutes or until sugar dissolves; bring to the boil. Remove from heat. Reserve ⅔ cup wine mixture. Return remaining wine mixture to the boil. Add blueberries; cook, uncovered, for 5 minutes or until wine mixture thickens and blueberries are heated through. Cover; refrigerate 2 hours or until cold.

rosewater raspberry cakes

PREP + COOK TIME 1½ HOURS (+ COOLING) • MAKES 12

You need 12 x 1¼-cup (310ml) straight-sided glass jars.

3 cups (450g) self-raising flour

250g (5½ ounces) butter, softened

1 teaspoon vanilla extract

1½ cups (330g) caster (superfine) sugar

6 eggs

½ cup (125ml) milk

rose pink food colouring

100g (3 ounces) pink rose-flavoured persian fairy floss (pashmak)

ROSEWATER CREAM

600ml thickened (heavy) cream

½ teaspoon rosewater

rose pink food colouring

Test Kitchen NOTES

Swap the butter cake for 2 x 340g (11-ounce) packets butter cake mix if you like. Make the cakes according to the packet directions.

1 Preheat oven to 180°C/350°F.

2 Sift flour into a small bowl of an electric mixer, add butter, extract, sugar, eggs and milk; beat with an electric mixer on low speed until ingredients are combined. Increase speed to medium; beat until mixture is changed to a paler colour.

3 Divide mixture into three medium bowls. Tint one bowl pale pink with food colouring. Tint another bowl a medium shade of pink. Tint remaining bowl a darker pink. Spoon dark pink cake mixture into a plastic disposable piping bag; snip end to make a 1cm (½-inch) opening. Pipe mixture evenly into bases of jars. Repeat with remaining mixtures and piping bags, finishing with the palest pink mixture.

4 Place jars in large deep baking dish; pour enough boiling water into baking dish to come 3cm (1¼ inches) up the sides of jars. Cover dish with foil. Place dish in oven; bake about 50 minutes. Remove jars from dish; cool.

5 Just before serving, make rosewater cream. Dollop rosewater cream on top of cooled cakes in jars; top with fairy floss.

rosewater cream Combine cream and rosewater in a medium bowl of an electric mixer; tint pink with food colouring (tint slightly darker than you want, as the colour will become slightly less intense once you whip it.) Beat mixture with an electric mixer until soft peaks form.

When piping the mixture into the jars, pipe around the edge first, then fill in the middle; this will give nice neat layers.

Test Kitchen
NOTES

Uniced cakes can be made a
day ahead or frozen for up to
three months. If icing is too
thick to spread add 1 teaspoon
of hot water until spreadable.

banana, peanut butter & bacon cupcakes

PREP + COOK TIME 1 HOUR (+ COOLING) • MAKES 12

You need 2 large (460g) overripe bananas to get the amount of mashed banana need for this recipe.

6 thin slices streaky bacon

2 tablespoons maple syrup

2 cups (300g) self-raising flour

¾ cup (165g) caster (superfine) sugar

¼ cup (60ml) milk

125g (4 ounces) butter, melted, cooled

2 eggs

1 teaspoon vanilla extract

1 cup (280g) mashed banana

PEANUT BUTTER FROSTING

125g (4 ounces) cream cheese, softened

½ cup (140g) smooth peanut butter

2½ cups (400g) icing (confectioners') sugar

2 tablespoons milk

1 Preheat oven to 200°C/400°F.

2 Place bacon on a wire rack set over an oven tray lined with foil. Brush with half the syrup. Bake about 20 minutes, turning halfway through cooking and basting with remaining syrup until crisp. Set aside to cool. Break into pieces.

3 Reduce oven temperature to 170°C/340°F. Line a 12-hole (⅓-cup/80ml) muffin pan with paper cases.

4 Combine sifted flour and sugar in a large bowl; make a well in the centre. Add combined milk, butter, eggs and extract; stir to combine. Stir in banana. Drop ¼-cups of mixture into paper cases.

5 Bake about 25 minutes. Stand cakes in pan for 5 minutes before turning, top-side up, onto a wire rack to cool.

6 Make peanut butter frosting. Fit a medium piping bag with a 2cm (¾-inch) star nozzle. Pipe frosting over cakes; top with bacon.

peanut butter frosting Beat cream cheese and peanut butter in a small bowl with an electric mixer until light and fluffy. Gradually beat in sifted icing sugar and milk, in two batches.

chocolate caramel crunch cakes

You need a large piping bag fitted with a large fluted tube.

60g (2 ounces) dark (semi-sweet) chocolate, chopped coarsely

⅔ cup (160ml) water

90g (3 ounces) butter, softened

1 cup (220g) firmly packed brown sugar

2 eggs

⅔ cup (100g) self-raising flour

2 tablespoons cocoa powder

⅓ cup (40g) ground almonds

¾ cup (180ml) good quality store-bought caramel sauce

¼ cup (35g) finely chopped salted peanuts

PEANUT BUTTER CREAM

¾ cup (210g) smooth or crunchy peanut butter

185g (6 ounces) butter, softened

1½ tablespoons milk

1¼ cups (200g) icing (confectioners') sugar

1 Preheat oven to 170°C/340°F. Line a 12-hole (⅓-cup/80ml) muffin pan with paper cases.

2 Stir chocolate and the water in a small saucepan over low heat until smooth.

3 Beat butter, sugar and eggs in a small bowl with an electric mixer until light and fluffy. Stir in sifted flour and cocoa, then ground almonds and warm chocolate mixture. Divide mixture evenly into paper cases.

4 Bake about 25 minutes. Stand cakes in pan for 5 minutes before turning, top-side up, onto a wire rack to cool.

5 Make peanut butter cream.

6 Cut a deep circle into the top of cold cakes; fill each hole with about 2 teaspoons of caramel sauce.

7 Spoon peanut butter cream into piping bag; pipe swirls over caramel filling. Drizzle with remaining caramel sauce; sprinkle with nuts.

peanut butter cream Beat peanut butter, butter and milk in a small bowl with an electric mixer until light and fluffy. Gradually beat in sifted icing sugar.

Unfilled, uniced cakes can be made a day ahead or frozen for up to three months.

Cakes can be made a day
ahead; layer just before
serving. Freeze unfilled cakes
for up to three months.

pistachio and pomegranate cakes

You need 6 x 1¼-cup (310ml) straight-sided glass jars.

¾ cup (105g) unsalted pistachios

125g (4 ounces) butter, softened

¾ cup (165g) caster (superfine) sugar

2 eggs

¾ cup (110g) self-raising flour

½ cup (125ml) buttermilk

green food colouring

⅓ cup (45g) coarsely chopped roasted pistachios

POMEGRANATE SYRUP

2 pomegranates (760g)

2 tablespoons caster (superfine) sugar

YOGHURT CREAM

300ml thickened (heavy) cream

1 cup (280g) thick greek-style yoghurt

2 tablespoons icing (confectioners') sugar

pink food colouring

1 Preheat oven to 180°C/350°F. Grease six 1¼-cup (310ml) straight-sided glass jars.

2 Process pistachios until fine. Beat butter and sugar in a small bowl with an electric mixer until light and fluffy; beat in eggs, one at a time. Transfer mixture to a large bowl; stir in ground nuts, sifted flour and buttermilk, in two batches. Tint mixture a pale green with food colouring. Divide mixture evenly into jars.

3 Place jars in large deep baking dish; pour enough boiling water into baking dish to come 3cm (1¼ inches) up the sides of jars. Cover with foil. Bake about 50 minutes. Remove jars from dish. Stand cakes in jars 5 minutes before turning, top-side up, onto wire racks to cool. Wipe jars clean.

4 Make pomegranate syrup.

5 Make yoghurt cream.

6 Split each cooled cake into 3 layers. Layer cakes and yoghurt cream in jars, finishing with yoghurt cream. Drizzle with pomegranate syrup; sprinkle with reserved pomegranate seeds and chopped pistachios.

pomegranate syrup Strain pomegranate pulp (seeds and juice) over a medium bowl. Reserve the juice and half the seeds separately (discard remaining seeds). Place the juice and sugar in a small saucepan; stir over low heat until sugar dissolves. Increase heat to high; bring to the boil. Reduce heat; simmer, uncovered, about 5 minutes or until syrup thickens slightly. Cool.

yoghurt cream Combine cream, yoghurt and sifted icing sugar in a medium bowl of an electric mixer; tint pink with food colouring (tint slightly darker than you want, as the colour will become slightly less intense once you whip it.) Beat mixture with an electric mixer until soft peaks form.

champagne cupcakes

PREP + COOK TIME 1½ HOURS (+ COOLING) • MAKES 48

Uniced cakes can be made a day ahead or frozen for up to three months.

125g (4 ounces) butter, softened

1 teaspoon vanilla extract

¾ cup (165g) caster (superfine) sugar

3 eggs

1½ cups (225g) self-raising flour

¼ cup (60ml) sparkling wine

pink sanding sugar, to decorate

pink soft sugar pearls, to decorate

CHAMPAGNE BUTTER CREAM

250g (8 ounces) butter, softened

3 cups (480g) icing (confectioners') sugar

¼ cup (60ml) sparkling wine

1 Preheat oven to 180°C/350°F. Line four 12-hole (1-tablespoon/20ml) mini muffin pans with pink paper cases.

2 Beat butter, extract, sugar, eggs, sifted flour and wine in a small bowl with an electric mixer on low speed until ingredients are combined. Increase speed to medium; beat until mixture has changed to a paler colour. Drop 2 level teaspoons of mixture into each paper case.

3 Bake about 12 minutes. Stand cakes in pan for 5 minutes before turning, top-side up, onto a wire rack to cool.

4 Make champagne butter cream.

5 Spoon butter cream into a large piping bag fitted with a large fluted tube. Pipe swirls of butter cream on top of each cake. Sprinkle with sanding sugar and sugar pearls.

champagne butter cream Beat butter in a small bowl with an electric mixer until as white as possible. Beat in sifted icing sugar and wine, in two batches.

beer & pretzel cakes with coffee cream

PREP + COOK TIME 1 HOUR (+ COOLING) • MAKES 12

You need a large piping bag fitted with a large plain tube.

125g (4 ounces) butter, softened
1 teaspoon vanilla extract
¾ cup (165g) firmly packed brown sugar
2 eggs
1¼ cups (185g) self-raising flour
½ cup (125ml) dark ale
12 whole small lightly salted pretzels

COFFEE BUTTER CREAM
185g (6 ounces) unsalted butter, softened
2¼ cups (360g) icing (confectioners') sugar
3 teaspoons coffee liqueur

1 Preheat oven to 170°C/340°F. Line a 12-hole (⅓-cup/80ml) muffin pan with paper cases.
2 Beat butter, extract, sugar, eggs, sifted flour and ale in a small bowl with an electric mixer on low speed until ingredients are combined. Increase speed to medium; beat until mixture has changed to a paler colour. Divide mixture evenly into paper cases.
3 Bake about 25 minutes. Stand cakes in pan for 5 minutes before turning, top-side up, onto a wire rack to cool.
4 Make coffee butter cream.
5 Spoon butter cream into a large piping bag fitted with a large plain tube. Pipe large swirls of butter cream onto cold cakes; top with pretzels.

coffee butter cream Beat butter in a small bowl with an electric mixer until as white as possible. Beat in half the sifted icing sugar and liqueur, in two batches.

Test Kitchen NOTES

Uniced cakes can be frozen for up to three months. Cakes can be iced a day ahead, store, in an airtight container, in the fridge; bring cakes to room temperature before serving.

Uniced cakes can be made a day ahead or frozen for up to three months. Ice cakes on the day of serving.

chocolate hearts

You need a 4cm (1½-inch) heart-shaped cutter.

1 cup (150g) self-raising flour

½ cup (75g) plain (all-purpose) flour

⅓ cup (35g) cocoa powder

¾ cup (165g) caster (superfine) sugar

185g (6 ounces) butter, softened

3 eggs

½ cup (125ml) milk

1 tablespoon icing (confectioners') sugar

RASPBERRY FROSTING

40g (1½ ounces) butter, softened

¼ cup (40g) frozen raspberries, thawed

1 cup (160g) icing (confectioners') sugar

1 Preheat oven to 180°C/350°F. Line a 12-hole (⅓-cup/80ml) muffin pan with paper cases.

2 Sift flours and cocoa into a large bowl of an electric mixer, add caster sugar, butter, eggs and milk; beat on low speed until ingredients are combined. Increase speed to medium; beat until mixture is smooth and has changed to a paler colour. Drop ¼ cups of mixture into paper cases.

3 Bake about 20 minutes. Stand cakes in pan for 5 minutes before turning, top-side up, onto a wire rack to cool.

4 Make raspberry frosting.

5 Carefully cut the top off each cupcake. Using the cutter, cut heart shapes from cake tops; reserve cake tops. Sprinkle heart shape with sifted icing sugar.

6 Spread 2 teaspoons of raspberry frosting over each cake. Replace cake tops, then top with hearts, using picture as a guide.

raspberry frosting Blend or process ingredients until smooth.

4 cupcake
ICE-CREAM SANDWICHES

MINTY CHOC-CHIP

Spread partially melted mint choc-chip ice-cream into a shallow pan; refreeze. Cut 12 cupcakes in half crossways. Place bases back into muffin pan. Cut ice-cream into 5.5cm (2¼-inch) rounds and sandwich between two cake halves. Place cakes in freezer for 15 minutes. Half-fill the piping bag with ganache. Pipe swirls of ganache on top of cakes; sprinkle ganache with 10 crushed pale-green sugared almonds.

DOUBLE CHOCOLATE

Spread partially melted chocolate chip ice-cream into a shallow pan; refreeze. Cut 12 cupcakes in half crossways. Place bases back into muffin pan. Cut ice-cream into 5.5cm (2¼-inch) rounds and sandwich between two cake halves. Place cakes in freezer for 15 minutes. Half-fill the piping bag with ganache. Pipe swirls of ganache on top of cakes; sprinkle with white chocolate curls.

Test Kitchen NOTES

You need 12 chocolate cupcakes for each of these recipes (see chocolate heart cake recipe, page 50) and 1½ quantities of dark chocolate ganache (see page 115) for each decorating technique. You also need a large piping bag fitted with a large fluted tube.

NEOPOLITAN

Spread partially melted neopolitan ice-cream into a shallow pan; refreeze. Cut 12 cupcakes in half crossways. Place bases back into muffin pan. Cut ice-cream into 5.5cm (2¼-inch) rounds and sandwich between two cake halves. Place cakes in freezer for 15 minutes. Half-fill the piping bag with ganache. Pipe swirls of ganache on top of cakes; sprinkle with pink cachous.

HOKEY POKEY

Spread partially melted hokey pokey ice-cream into a shallow pan; refreeze. Cut 12 cupcakes in half crossways. Place bases back into muffin pan. Cut ice-cream into 5.5cm (2¼-inch) rounds and sandwich between two cake halves. Place cakes in freezer for 15 minutes. Half-fill the piping bag with ganache. Pipe swirls of ganache on top of cakes; sprinkle with granulated (chopped) nuts.

chocolate cream cake pots

PREP + COOK TIME 2 HOURS (+ STANDING & COOLING) • MAKES 6

You need six 1¼-cup (310ml) straight-sided glass jars.

90g (3 ounces) dark (semi-sweet) chocolate, chopped coarsely

2 tablespoons dutch-processed cocoa powder

¾ cup (180ml) boiling water

125g (4 ounces) unsalted butter, softened

2 eggs

1 cup (220g) firmly packed brown sugar

⅓ cup (80g) sour cream

¾ cup (110g) plain (all-purpose) flour

½ cup (75g) self-raising flour

½ teaspoon bicarbonate of soda (baking soda)

300ml thickened (heavy) cream

150g (4½ ounces) almond nougat, chopped coarsely

DARK CHOCOLATE GANACHE

90g (3 ounces) dark (semi-sweet) chocolate, chopped finely

¼ cup (60ml) pouring cream

1 Preheat oven to 180°C/350°F. Grease six 1¼-cup (310ml) straight-sided glass jars.

2 Stir chocolate, sifted cocoa powder and the water in a small saucepan, over low heat, until smooth. Transfer mixture to a large bowl of an electric mixer; cool 10 minutes.

3 Add butter, eggs, sugar, sour cream and sifted flours and soda to the chocolate mixture; beat with an electric mixer, on low speed, until combined. Increase speed to medium; beat about 2 minutes or until mixture is smooth and changed to a paler colour. Divide mixture into jars.

4 Place jars in a large deep baking dish; pour enough boiling water into baking dish to come 3cm (1¼ inches) up the sides of jars. Cover with foil; bake about 50 minutes. Remove jars from dish. Cool cakes in jars.

5 Meanwhile, make dark chocolate ganache.

6 Beat cream in a small bowl with an electric mixer until soft peaks form.

7 Serve cakes in jars topped with a dollop of cream. Drizzle with ganache; top with nougat.

dark chocolate ganache Stir chocolate and cream in a small heatproof bowl over a small saucepan of simmering water until smooth. Cool.

Uniced cakes can be made a day ahead. Top with cream and ganache just before serving.

lemonade cupcakes with blackberry swirl frosting

PREP + COOK TIME 1 HOUR (+ COOLING) · MAKES 12

125g (4 ounces) butter, softened

½ cup (110g) caster (superfine) sugar

1 tablespoon finely grated lemon rind

2 eggs

1½ cups (225g) self-raising flour

½ cup (125ml) lemonade

12 frozen or fresh blackberries

BLACKBERRY SWIRL FROSTING

¼ cup (35g) frozen blackberries, thawed

500g (1 pound) cream cheese, softened

2 cups (320g) icing (confectioners') sugar

1 tablespoon lemonade

2 teaspoons finely grated lemon rind

1 Preheat oven to 180°C/350°F. Line a 12-hole (⅓-cup/80ml) muffin pan with paper cases.

2 Meanwhile, make blackberry swirl frosting.

3 Beat butter, sugar and rind in a small bowl with an electric mixer until light and fluffy. Beat in eggs, one at a time. Transfer mixture to a large bowl; stir in sifted flour and lemonade, in two batches. Divide mixture evenly into paper cases.

4 Bake about 20 minutes. Stand cupcakes in pans 5 minutes before turning, top-side up, onto wire racks to cool.

5 Using a small ice-cream scoop, scoop frosting and place on top of cupcakes.

blackberry swirl frosting Crush berries very well with a fork. Beat cream cheese, sifted icing sugar, lemonade and rind in a small bowl with an electric mixer until smooth. Lightly fold crushed blackberries through cream cheese mixture to create a swirled effect (don't over-mix or you will lose the swirl). Place frosting in the freezer for a few hours or until firm.

Test Kitchen
NOTES

You need 4 large piping bags
fitted with 2cm (¾-inch) plain
tubes for this recipe. Or put
the frosting in a large strong
plastic bag and cut a 1cm tip
from the corner. Uniced cakes
can be made a day ahead or
frozen for up to three months.

Substitute coconut cream for the liqueur, if you like.

pina colada cupcakes

PREP + COOK TIME 1¼ HOURS (+ COOLING) • MAKES 12

90g (3 ounces) butter, softened

1 teaspoon vanilla extract

2 tablespoons coconut liqueur

½ cup (110g) caster (superfine) sugar

2 eggs

1 cup (150g) self-raising flour

2 tablespoons coconut cream

440g (14 ounces) canned crushed pineapple in juice, drained

⅔ cup (30g) shredded coconut

COCONUT CREAM CHEESE FROSTING

60g (2 ounces) butter, softened

90g (3 ounces) cream cheese, softened

¼ cup (60ml) coconut liqueur

2½ cups (400g) icing (confectioners') sugar

green food colouring

1 Preheat oven to 180°C/350°F. Line a 12-hole (⅓-cup/80ml) muffin pan with paper cases.

2 Beat butter, extract, liqueur, sugar, eggs, sifted flour and coconut cream in a small bowl with an electric mixer on low speed until ingredients are combined. Increase speed to medium; beat until mixture has changed to a paler colour. Stir in pineapple. Drop ¼-cups of mixture into paper cases.

3 Bake about 25 minutes. Stand cakes in pan for 5 minutes before turning, top-side up, onto a wire rack to cool.

4 Make coconut cream cheese frosting; pipe each frosting onto 3 cakes. Top with shredded coconut.

coconut cream cheese frosting Beat butter, cream cheese and liqueur in a small bowl with an electric mixer until light and fluffy. Gradually beat in sifted icing sugar. Divide frosting into 4 small bowls; tint three bowls of frosting pale, light and medium green using colouring. Leave the remaining bowl plain.

peach melba cakes

You need six 1-cup (250ml) straight-sided glass jars.

90g (3 ounces) butter, softened

1 vanilla bean, cut in half lengthways, seeds scraped

½ cup (110g) caster (superfine) sugar

2 eggs

1 cup (150g) self-raising flour

2 tablespoons milk

¾ cup (180ml) thickened (heavy) cream

2 medium peaches (300g), sliced thinly

1½ tablespoons flaked almonds, toasted

RASPBERRY SAUCE

1 cup (150g) frozen raspberries

¼ cup (55g) caster (superfine) sugar

1 Preheat oven to 180°C/350°F. Grease six 1-cup (250ml) glass jars.

2 Beat butter, vanilla seeds, sugar, eggs, sifted flour and milk in a small bowl with an electric mixer on low speed until ingredients are combined. Increase speed to medium; beat until mixture has changed to a paler colour. Drop ⅓-cups of mixture into jars.

3 Place jars in a large baking dish. Pour boiling water into baking dish until water comes halfway up sides of jars. Bake about 40 minutes. Remove jars from dish; cool cakes in jars.

4 Meanwhile, make raspberry sauce.

5 Whip cream in a small bowl until soft peaks form.

6 Top cold cakes evenly with raspberry sauce, then dollops of cream, peach slices and almonds.

raspberry sauce Heat raspberries and sugar in a small saucepan over low heat for 2 minutes or until sugar dissolves. Increase heat to medium; cook, stirring, for 2 minutes or until raspberries start to break down and sauce thickens. Cover; refrigerate for 30 minutes or until cold.

Test Kitchen
NOTES

Uniced cakes can be made a day ahead; store at room temperature. Raspberry sauce can be made a day ahead, store, covered, in the fridge. If peaches aren't in season replace with 400g (12½ ounces) canned peaches, drained.

Cakes are best made on day of serving.

honey and lavender cakes

You need a large piping bag fitted with a 2cm (¾-inch) plain tube.

1½ teaspoons culinary lavender

3 eggs

¼ cup (55g) caster (superfine) sugar

¼ cup (40g) icing (confectioner's) sugar

½ cup (75g) self-raising flour

⅓ cup (50g) plain (all-purpose) flour

100g (3 ounces) butter, melted

2 tablespoons hot water

fresh organic lavender, to decorate

HONEY FROSTING

90g (3 ounces) butter, softened

⅓ cup (80g) sour cream

1 tablespoon honey

1½ cups (240g) icing (confectioner's) sugar

1 Preheat oven to 180°C/350°F. Line a 12-hole (⅓-cup/80ml) muffin pan with paper cases.

2 Using a mortar and pestle, grind lavender until fine. Beat eggs, caster sugar and sifted icing sugar in a small bowl with an electric mixer for 5 minutes or until thick and creamy.

3 Sift flours twice on a piece of baking paper, then sift over egg mixture, add lavender. Pour combined butter and the water down side of bowl, then fold ingredients together with a large metal spoon. Pour ¼-cups of mixture into paper cases.

4 Bake about 15 minutes. Stand cupcakes in pans for 5 minutes before turning, top-side up, onto wire racks to cool.

5 Meanwhile, make honey frosting.

6 Spoon frosting into piping bag; pipe swirls of frosting onto cakes. Sprinkle with fresh lavender.

honey frosting Beat butter, sour cream, honey and sifted icing sugar in a small bowl with electric mixer until smooth; do not overbeat.

family favourites

carrot cake with lemon cream cheese frosting

PREP + COOK TIME 1¾ HOURS • SERVES 12

3 eggs

1⅓ cups (250g) firmly packed brown sugar

1 cup (250ml) vegetable oil

3 cups coarsely grated carrot

1 cup (120g) coarsely chopped walnuts

2½ cups (375g) self-raising flour

½ teaspoon bicarbonate of soda (baking soda)

2 teaspoons mixed spice

LEMON CREAM CHEESE FROSTING

65g (2 ounces) butter, softened

165g (5 ounces) cream cheese, softened

2¼ teaspoons finely grated lemon rind

3⅓ cups (540g) icing (confectioners') sugar

1 Preheat oven to 180°C/350°F. Grease a deep 22cm (9-inch) round cake pan; line base with baking paper.

2 Beat eggs, sugar and oil in a small bowl with an electric mixer until thick and creamy. Transfer mixture to a large bowl; stir in carrot and nuts, then sifted dry ingredients. Pour mixture into pan.

3 Bake about 1¼ hours. Stand cake in pan for 5 minutes before turning, top-side up, onto a wire rack to cool.

4 Meanwhile, make lemon cream cheese frosting.

5 Split cake in half; spread bottom layer with half the frosting. Top with remaining layer; spread top with remaining frosting. Top with caramelised walnuts, if you like (see step 2, page 67).

lemon cream cheese frosting Beat butter, cream cheese and rind in a small bowl with an electric mixer until light and fluffy. Gradually beat in sifted icing sugar.

This cake is best eaten the day it is made.

coffee and walnut cake

PREP + COOK TIME 1¼ HOURS (+ COOLING & STANDING) • SERVES 8

30g (1 ounce) butter

1 tablespoon brown sugar

2 teaspoons ground cinnamon

2 cups (200g) roasted walnuts

½ cup (125ml) milk

1 tablespoon instant coffee granules

185g (6 ounces) butter, softened, extra

1⅓ cups (300g) caster (superfine) sugar

3 eggs

1 cup (150g) self-raising flour

¾ cup (110g) plain (all-purpose) flour

TOFFEE DRIZZLE

½ cup (110g) caster (superfine) sugar

2 tablespoons water

3 teaspoons pouring cream

1 Preheat oven to 160°C/325°F. Grease a 22cm (9-inch) baba cake pan well (see page 113); dust with flour, shake out excess.

2 Melt butter in a small saucepan over medium heat; stir in brown sugar, cinnamon and nuts. Cool.

3 Combine milk and coffee in a small bowl; stir until coffee dissolves.

4 Beat extra butter and caster sugar in a small bowl with an electric mixer until light and fluffy. Beat in eggs, one at a time. Stir in sifted flours, then milk mixture.

5 Spread one-third of the cake mixture into base of pan; sprinkle with half the nut mixture. Top with remaining cake mixture. Bake about 45 minutes. Stand cake in pan for 5 minutes before turning onto a wire rack over an oven tray to cool.

6 Make toffee drizzle.

7 Working quickly, drizzle some of the toffee over top of cake, press on remaining nut mixture; drizzle with remaining toffee.

toffee drizzle Stir sugar and the water in a small saucepan over medium heat, without boiling, until sugar dissolves; bring to the boil. Reduce heat; simmer, uncovered, without stirring, until toffee becomes caramel in colour. Add cream; stir for 1 minute or until thickened slightly.

rhubarb frangipane cake

PREP + COOK TIME 2 HOURS (+ COOLING) • SERVES 15

2 bunches rhubarb (1kg)

¼ cup (55g) caster (superfine) sugar

2 tablespoons caster (superfine) sugar, extra

1 vanilla bean pod, split lengthways

¼ cup (60ml) water

250g (8 ounces) butter, softened

2 teaspoons vanilla extract

1 cup (220g) caster (superfine) sugar, extra

3 eggs

½ cup (120g) sour cream

1 cup (120g) ground almonds

1 cup (150g) self-raising flour

½ cup (75g) plain (all-purpose) flour

greek-style plain yoghurt, to serve

FRANGIPANE

60g (2 ounces) butter, softened

1 egg

⅓ cup (75g) caster (superfine) sugar

1 cup (120g) ground almonds

2 tablespoons brandy

1 Preheat oven to 180°C/350°F. Grease a deep 22cm (9-inch) square cake pan; line base and sides with baking paper.

2 Trim rhubarb; cut into 12cm (5-inch) lengths. Cut thick stems in half lengthways so stems are about the same thickness to help them cook evenly. Toss rhubarb with sugar in a shallow baking dish. Roast rhubarb, uncovered, for 20 minutes or until tender. Drain rhubarb; reserve syrup in dish. Cool.

3 Meanwhile, place extra sugar, vanilla pod, the water and reserved syrup in a small saucepan. Cook, stirring, over medium heat, until sugar is dissolved. Reduce heat; simmer, without stirring, for 5 minutes or until syrup is thickened slightly.

4 Make frangipane.

5 Beat butter, extract and extra sugar in a small bowl with an electric mixer until light and fluffy. Beat in eggs, one at a time, then beat in sour cream.

6 Transfer mixture to a large bowl; stir in ground almonds and sifted flours. Spread mixture into pan. Spread frangipane over cake batter, top with rhubarb.

7 Bake about 1 hour. Stand cake in pan for 10 minutes before turning, top-side up, onto a wire rack. Brush warm cake with reserved rhubarb syrup. Dollop with yoghurt to serve, if you like.

frangipane Beat butter, egg and sugar in a small bowl with an electric mixer until creamy. Stir in ground almonds and brandy.

Test Kitchen
NOTES

Cake is best made on the day of serving. Store leftovers covered in the refrigerator; warm cake before serving.

This cake will keep in an airtight container for up to three days. Uniced cake can be frozen for up to three months.

caramel butter cake

PREP + COOK TIME 1¼ HOURS · SERVES 10

125g (4 ounces) butter, softened

1 cup (220g) firmly packed brown sugar

1 teaspoon vanilla extract

2 eggs

1 tablespoon golden syrup or treacle

1 cup (150g) plain (all-purpose) flour

½ cup (75g) self-raising flour

1 teaspoon ground cinnamon

½ cup (125ml) milk

CARAMEL ICING

1½ cups (330g) firmly packed brown sugar

90g (3 ounces) butter

2½ tablespoons milk

1¼ cups (200g) icing (confectioners') sugar

3 teaspoons milk, extra

1 Preheat oven to 180°C/350°F. Grease a deep 20cm (8-inch) round cake pan; line base with baking paper.

2 Beat butter, sugar and extract in a small bowl with an electric mixer until light and fluffy. Beat in eggs and golden syrup. Stir in sifted flours and cinnamon, and milk in two batches. Spread mixture into pan.

3 Bake cake for 50 minutes or until a skewer inserted into the centre comes out clean. Stand cake in pan for 5 minutes before turning, top-side up, onto a wire rack to cool.

4 Meanwhile, make caramel icing. Spread icing on top of cold cake before serving.

caramel icing Heat brown sugar, butter and milk in a small saucepan, stirring constantly, over medium heat, without boiling until sugar dissolves. Bring to the boil. Reduce heat; simmer, uncovered, 3 minutes without stirring. Remove from heat; stir in sifted icing sugar. Stir in extra milk until icing is of a spreadable consistency.

passionfruit featherlight sponge

PREP + COOK TIME 40 MINUTES • SERVES 10

4 eggs

¾ cup (165g) caster (superfine) sugar

⅔ cup (150g) wheaten cornflour (cornstarch)

¼ cup (30g) custard powder

1 teaspoon cream of tartar

½ teaspoon bicarbonate of soda (baking soda)

300ml thickened (heavy) cream

2 teaspoons icing (confectioners') sugar

2 passionfruit

1 tablespoon icing (confectioners') sugar, extra

1 Preheat oven to 200°C/400°F. Grease and flour two deep 22cm (9-inch) round cake pans; shake out the excess flour.

2 Beat eggs and sugar in a small bowl with an electric mixer for 7 minutes or until thick and creamy. Transfer mixture to a large bowl.

3 Sift dry ingredients twice onto a piece of baking paper. Sift flour mixture a third time evenly over egg mixture. Using a balloon whisk or large metal spoon, quickly and lightly fold flour mixture through egg mixture until incorporated.

4 Pour mixture evenly into pans; tilt pans to spread mixture to the edge.

5 Bake cakes for 20 minutes or until they spring back when pressed lightly in the centre. Turn cakes immediately, top-side up, onto baking-paper-covered wire racks. Cool.

6 Beat cream and sugar in a small bowl with an electric mixer until soft peaks form; fold in passionfruit pulp.

7 Sandwich sponges with passionfruit cream. Dust with sifted icing sugar, to serve.

orange poppy seed syrup cake

⅓ cup (50g) poppy seeds

¼ cup (60ml) milk

185g (6 ounces) butter, softened

1 tablespoon finely grated orange rind

1 cup (220g) caster (superfine) sugar

3 eggs

1½ cups (225g) self-raising flour

½ cup (75g) plain (all-purpose) flour

½ cup (60g) ground almonds

½ cup (125ml) orange juice

ORANGE SYRUP

1 cup (220g) caster (superfine) sugar

⅔ cup (160ml) orange juice

⅓ cup (80ml) water

1 Combine seeds and milk in a small bowl; stand for 20 minutes.

2 Preheat oven to 180°C/350°F. Grease a deep 22cm (9-inch) round cake pan; line base and side with baking paper.

3 Beat butter, rind and sugar in a small bowl with an electric mixer until light and fluffy; beat in eggs, one at a time. Transfer mixture to a large bowl; using a wooden spoon, stir in sifted flours, ground almonds, juice and poppy-seed mixture. Spread mixture into pan; bake about 1 hour.

4 Meanwhile, make orange syrup.

5 Stand cake in pan for 5 minutes before turning, top-side up, onto a wire rack set over tray. Pour hot syrup over hot cake; serve warm.

orange syrup Using a wooden spoon, stir ingredients in a small saucepan over heat, without boiling, until sugar dissolves. Bring to the boil; reduce heat, simmer, uncovered, without stirring, for 2 minutes.

hummingbird cake

You need two large overripe (460g) bananas for this recipe.

450g (14½ ounces) canned crushed pineapple in syrup

1 cup (150g) plain (all-purpose) flour

½ cup (75g) self-raising flour

½ teaspoon bicarbonate of soda (baking soda)

½ teaspoon each ground cinnamon and ginger

1 cup (220g) firmly packed brown sugar

½ cup (40g) desiccated coconut

1 cup mashed banana

2 eggs, beaten lightly

¾ cup (180ml) vegetable oil

PINEAPPLE IN SYRUP

2 tablespoons caster (superfine) sugar

½ cup (125ml) water

1 small pineapple (900g), peeled, halved, sliced thinly

CREAM CHEESE FROSTING

60g (2 ounces) butter, softened

120g (4 ounces) cream cheese, softened

2 teaspoons vanilla extract

3 cups (480g) icing (confectioners') sugar

1 Make pineapple in syrup.

2 Preheat oven to 180°C/350°F. Grease a deep 23cm (9-inch) square cake pan; line base with baking paper.

3 Drain pineapple over a medium bowl, pressing with a spoon to extract as much syrup as possible. Reserve ¼ cup of the syrup.

4 Sift flours, soda, spices and sugar into a large bowl. Using a wooden spoon, stir in drained pineapple, reserved syrup, coconut, banana, egg and oil.

5 Pour mixture into pan; bake about 40 minutes. Stand cake in pan for 5 minutes before turning, top-side up, onto a wire rack to cool.

6 Meanwhile, make cream cheese frosting; spread cake with frosting. Top with pineapple slices. Drizzle with a little syrup.

pineapple in syrup Stir sugar and the water in a small saucepan over medium heat, without boiling, until sugar dissolves. Bring to the boil, then reduce heat to a simmer (do not stir). Add pineapple slices, in batches; cook, without stirring, for 4 minutes or until softened. Transfer to a plate to cool. Repeat with remaining pineapple. Reserve syrup.

cream cheese frosting Beat butter, cream cheese and extract in a small bowl with an electric mixer until light and fluffy. Gradually beat in sifted icing sugar.

dark gingerbread cake

125g (4 ounces) butter, softened

½ cup (110g) firmly packed dark brown sugar

2 eggs

1⅔ cups (250g) plain (all-purpose) flour

½ teaspoon bicarbonate of soda (baking soda)

2 teaspoons ground ginger

1 cup (360g) treacle

2 tablespoons milk

¼ cup (55g) finely chopped glacé ginger

⅓ cup (55g) finely chopped raisins

strips of lemon rind and sliced crystallised ginger, to decorate

LEMON GLACÉ ICING

2 cups (320g) icing (confectioners') sugar

20g (¾ ounce) butter, softened

2 tablespoons lemon juice

1 Preheat oven to 180°C/350°F. Grease a 20cm x 30cm (8-inch x 12-inch) rectangular cake pan; line base and sides with baking paper, extending the paper 5cm (2 inches) above sides.

2 Beat butter and sugar in a small bowl with an electric mixer until light and fluffy. Beat in eggs, one at a time. Transfer mixture to a large bowl; stir in sifted flour, soda and ground ginger, treacle, milk, glacé ginger and raisins. Spread mixture into pan.

3 Bake about 45 minutes or until a skewer inserted into the centre comes out clean. Stand cake in pan for 5 minutes before turning, top-side up, onto a wire rack to cool.

4 Meanwhile, make lemon glacé icing.

5 Spread cold cake with icing; stand until icing is set. Sprinkle with lemon and ginger before cutting.

lemon glacé icing Sift icing sugar into a medium bowl. Stir in butter and juice until icing is smooth and spreadable.

mango coconut cake

250g (8 ounces) butter, softened

1 teaspoon coconut essence

1½ cups (330g) caster (superfine) sugar

4 eggs

⅔ cup (160ml) mango puree

2 cups (180g) desiccated coconut

2½ cups (375g) self-raising flour

COCONUT FROSTING

1 egg white

1¼ cups (200g) icing (confectioners') sugar

2 teaspoons mango puree

¾ cup (65g) desiccated coconut

½ cup (125g) mascarpone cheese

1 Preheat oven to 180°C/350°F. Grease a deep 22cm (9-inch) round cake pan; line base with baking paper.

2 Beat butter, essence and sugar in a small bowl with an electric mixer until combined. Add eggs, one at a time, beating only until combined between additions.

3 Transfer mixture to a large bowl. Using a wooden spoon, stir in puree and coconut, then sifted flour. Spread mixture into pan.

4 Bake about 1¼ hours. Stand cake in pan for 5 minutes before turning, top-side up, onto a wire rack to cool.

5 Meanwhile, make coconut frosting; spread cold cake with frosting.

coconut frosting Beat egg white in a small bowl with an electric mixer until foamy. Gradually beat in sifted icing sugar, 1 tablespoon at a time. Using a fork, mix in puree, coconut and mascarpone. Cover frosting with plastic wrap until required, pressing plastic directly onto surface to stop it drying out.

chocolate velvet cake

125g (4 ounces) butter, softened

1 cup (220g) firmly packed brown sugar

½ cup (110g) caster (superfine) sugar

3 eggs

2 cups (300g) plain (all-purpose) flour

⅓ cup (35g) cocoa powder

1 teaspoon bicarbonate of soda (baking soda)

⅔ cup (160g) sour cream

½ cup (125ml) water

1 cup (150g) sugared almonds, crushed coarsely

CHOCOLATE ICING

135g (4 ounces) dark (semi-sweet) chocolate, chopped coarsely

90g (3 ounces) butter, chopped coarsely

¾ cup (120g) icing (confectioners') sugar

⅓ cup (80g) sour cream

1 Preheat oven to 180°C/350°F. Grease a deep 23cm x 30cm (9-inch x 12-inch) rectangular cake pan or baking dish; line base and sides with baking paper, extending the paper 5cm (2 inches) above long sides.

2 Beat all ingredients, except sugared almonds, in a large bowl with an electric mixer on low speed until just combined. Increase speed to medium; beat for 3 minutes or until mixture is smooth and paler in colour. Spread mixture into pan or dish.

3 Bake for 45 minutes or until a skewer inserted into the centre comes out clean. Stand cake in pan for 10 minutes before turning, top-side up, onto a wire rack to cool.

4 Meanwhile, make chocolate icing.

5 Spread cold cake with chocolate icing; sprinkle with sugared almonds. Stand until set before cutting.

chocolate icing Stir ingredients in a small saucepan over low heat until smooth; cook, stirring, for a further 2 minutes. Transfer to a small bowl; cool 10 minutes. Refrigerate for 20 minutes or until icing is spreadable.

chocolate sponge roll

PREP + COOK TIME 30 MINUTES (+ COOLING) • SERVES 10

4 eggs, separated

½ cup (110g) caster (superfine) sugar

2 tablespoons hot water

60g (2 ounces) dark (semi-sweet) chocolate, grated coarsely

½ cup (75g) self-raising flour

2 tablespoons caster (superfine) sugar, extra

150g (4½ ounces) dark (semi-sweet) chocolate, melted (see page 112), cooled slightly

250g (1 punnet) fresh raspberries, to decorate

RASPBERRY VANILLA CREAM

1½ cups (375ml) thickened (heavy) cream

1 tablespoon icing (confectioners') sugar

2 teaspoons vanilla extract

1 cup fresh or frozen raspberries, pureed

1 Preheat oven to 180°C/350°F. Grease a 23cm x 32cm (9-inch x 13-inch) swiss roll pan; line base and long sides with baking paper, extending the paper 5cm (2 inches) over sides.

2 Beat egg yolks and sugar in a small bowl with an electric mixer about 5 minutes or until thick and creamy. Transfer mixture to a large bowl; fold in the hot water and chocolate, then fold in sifted flour.

3 Beat egg whites in a small bowl with an electric mixer until soft peaks form; fold into chocolate mixture. Spread mixture into pan. Bake cake about 12 minutes.

4 Meanwhile, place a piece of baking paper cut the same size as the pan on bench; sprinkle with extra sugar.

5 Turn hot sponge onto the sugared paper; peel away lining paper (see page 112). Using paper as a guide, loosely roll sponge from long side. Stand 2 minutes; unroll. Cool; trim all sides of sponge.

6 Make raspberry vanilla cream. Spread sponge with cream. Using paper as a guide, roll sponge up from long side. Drizzle roll with melted chocolate; sprinkle with raspberries. Stand until chocolate sets.

raspberry vanilla cream Beat cream, sifted icing sugar and extract in a small bowl with an electric mixer until soft peaks form. Fold through puree.

Test Kitchen NOTES

Filled sponge roll is best eaten the day it is made; store in an airtight container, in the fridge, until ready to serve.

4 ways with
CHOCOLATE BARS

MALTESERS

Half-fill the piping bag with whipped milk chocolate ganache (see page 115 on how to whip ganache). Pipe a swirl of ganache on top of each chocolate cupcake. Decorate with chopped Maltesers.

MARS BAR

Fold a finely chopped Mars Bar through white chocolate ganache. Half-fill the piping bag with ganache. Pipe a swirl of ganache on top of each chocolate cupcake. Top with extra coarsely chopped Mars Bar.

JUNIOR MINTS

Half-fill the piping bag with whipped milk chocolate ganache (see page 115 on how to whip ganache). Pipe a swirl of ganache on top of each chocolate cupcake. Dust lightly with sifted cocoa powder and decorate with Junior Mints.

SNICKERS

Partially melt a finely chopped Snickers bar in a microwave-safe bowl in a microwave oven on low power, in short bursts. Fold through the white chocolate ganache. Half-fill the piping bag with ganache. Pipe a swirl of ganache on top of each chocolate cupcake. Decorate with a drizzle of bottled caramel sauce and a sprinkle of granulated nuts.

passionfruit cake with orange blossom and mint tea syrup

PREP + COOK TIME 1¾ HOURS (+ STANDING & COOLING) • SERVES 8

220g (7 ounces) unsalted butter, softened

1 cup (220g) caster (superfine) sugar

3 eggs

2 cups (300g) self-raising flour

⅔ cup (160ml) buttermilk

⅓ cup (80ml) passionfruit pulp

1 tablespoon organic edible flowers (optional)

ORANGE BLOSSOM AND MINT TEA SYRUP

1 peppermint tea bag

1 cup (250ml) boiling water

1 cup (220g) caster (superfine) sugar

½ cup (125ml) passionfruit pulp

1 teaspoon orange blossom water

1 Make orange blossom and mint tea syrup.

2 Preheat oven to 180°C/350°F. Grease a 12cm x 23cm (4¾-inch x 9¼-inch) loaf pan; line base with baking paper.

3 Beat butter and sugar in a medium bowl with an electric mixer for 6 minutes or until pale and fluffy. Beat in eggs, one at a time. Fold in sifted flour, then buttermilk in two batches; fold in passionfruit until just combined. Spoon mixture into pan; smooth surface.

4 Bake for 50 minutes or until a skewer inserted into the centre comes out clean. Stand cake in pan for 10 minutes before turning, top-side up, onto a wire rack to cool.

5 Place cake on a plate; spoon half the syrup over the cake. Decorate with flowers. Serve cake with remaining syrup.

orange blossom and mint tea syrup Place tea bag in a small saucepan, pour over the boiling water; stand for 5 minutes. Squeeze liquid from tea bag; discard bag. Add sugar and passionfruit pulp to tea; stir over low heat until sugar dissolves. Increase heat to high, bring to the boil; boil for 15 minutes or until thick and syrupy. Remove from heat; stir in orange blossom water. Cool.

banana cake with passionfruit icing

PREP + COOK TIME 1½ HOURS • SERVES 10

Test Kitchen
NOTES

Cake can be made two days ahead, store in an airtight container. Uniced cake can be frozen for up to three months.

You need two large overripe bananas (460g) and two large passionfruit for this recipe.

125g (4 ounces) butter, softened

¾ cup (165g) firmly packed brown sugar

2 eggs

1½ cups (225g) self-raising flour

½ teaspoon bicarbonate of soda (baking soda)

1 teaspoon mixed spice

1 cup mashed banana

½ cup (120g) sour cream

¼ cup (60ml) milk

PASSIONFRUIT ICING

2¼ cups (360g) icing (confectioners') sugar

2 teaspoons softened butter

3 tablespoons passionfruit pulp

1 Preheat oven to 180°C/350°F. Grease 15cm x 25cm (6-inch x 10-inch) loaf pan; line base with baking paper.

2 Beat butter and sugar in a small bowl with an electric mixer until light and fluffy. Beat in eggs, one at a time. Transfer to a large bowl; stir in sifted dry ingredients, banana, sour cream and milk.

3 Spread mixture into pan; bake about 50 minutes. Stand cake in pan for 5 minutes before turning, top-side up, onto a wire rack to cool.

4 Meanwhile, make passionfruit icing. Spread cooled cake with icing.

passionfruit icing Combine ingredients in a medium bowl; stir until smooth.

boiled pineapple rum cake

PREP + COOK TIME 1½ HOURS (+ COOLING TIME) • SERVES 20

450g (14½ ounces) canned crushed pineapple in syrup

5 cups (1kg) mixed dried fruit

250g (8 ounces) butter, chopped coarsely

1 cup (220g) firmly packed brown sugar

2 tablespoons orange marmalade

2 tablespoons dark rum

4 eggs, beaten lightly

1⅔ cups (250g) plain (all-purpose) flour

⅓ cup (50g) self-raising flour

½ teaspoon bicarbonate of soda (baking soda)

1 tablespoon dark rum, extra

candied pineapple, to decorate (optional)

1 Drain pineapple over a large jug; discard ½ cup (125ml) of the syrup.

2 Combine pineapple, remaining syrup, fruit, butter, sugar, marmalade and rum in a large saucepan. Using a wooden spoon, stir over medium heat until butter melts and sugar dissolves; bring to the boil. Reduce heat; simmer, covered, for 10 minutes. Cool to room temperature.

3 Preheat oven to 150°C/300°F. Line base and side of a deep 20cm (8-inch) round cake pan with three thicknesses of baking paper, extending paper 5cm (2 inches) above edges.

4 Using a wooden spoon, stir egg and sifted dry ingredients into fruit mixture. Pour mixture into pan; bake about 2 hours.

5 Brush hot cake with extra rum. Cover pan tightly with foil; cool cake in pan.

Test Kitchen NOTES

Cake can be made one month ahead; store in an airtight container. Cover cake with foil while cooking to prevent it from over-browning.

Test Kitchen
NOTES

Cake can be made three days
ahead; store in an airtight
container. Cake can be frozen
for up to three months.

lumberjack cake

PREP + COOK TIME 1¾ HOURS • SERVES 12

2 large apples (400g), peeled, cored,
chopped finely

1 cup (150g) finely chopped seeded dried dates

1 teaspoon bicarbonate of soda (baking soda)

1 cup (250ml) boiling water

125g (4 ounces) butter, softened

1 teaspoon vanilla extract

1 cup (220g) caster (superfine) sugar

1 egg

1½ cups (225g) plain (all-purpose) flour

flaked fresh coconut, to decorate, optional

COCONUT TOPPING

60g (2 ounces) butter, chopped

½ cup (110g) firmly packed brown sugar

½ cup (125ml) milk

⅔ cup (50g) shredded coconut

1 Preheat oven to 180°C/350°F. Grease a deep
23cm (9-inch) square cake pan; line base and sides
with baking paper.
2 Combine apple, dates and soda in a large bowl,
stir in the water; cover bowl with plastic wrap, stand
for 10 minutes.
3 Meanwhile, beat butter, extract, sugar and egg in
a small bowl with an electric mixer until light and
fluffy. Add butter mixture to apple mixture; stir to
combine. Stir in sifted flour. Pour mixture into pan;
bake about 50 minutes.
4 Meanwhile, make coconut topping.
5 Remove cake carefully from oven to bench. Using
a metal spatula, carefully spread warm topping evenly
over cake; return to oven, bake a further 20 minutes
or until topping is browned.
6 Stand cake in pan for 5 minutes before turning,
top-side up, onto a wire rack to cool. Sprinkle with
flaked coconut just before serving, if you like.

coconut topping Combine ingredients in a medium
saucepan; using a wooden spoon, stir mixture over
low heat until butter melts and sugar dissolves.

sweet comfort

sticky toffee date puddings

PREP + COOK TIME 35 MINUTES • SERVES 8

250g (8 ounces) seeded dried dates

1¼ cups (310ml) water

1 teaspoon bicarbonate of soda (baking soda)

90g (3 ounces) butter, softened

2 eggs

¾ cup (165g) caster (superfine) sugar

2 teaspoons vanilla extract

1¼ cups (185g) plain (all-purpose) flour

TOFFEE SAUCE

1 cup (220g) caster (superfine) sugar

300ml pouring cream

1 Preheat oven to 180°C/350°F. Grease an 8-hole (½-cup/125ml) mini fluted tube pan.
2 Using scissors, coarsely cut the dates into a medium saucepan; add the water. Bring to the boil; remove from heat, stir in soda. Cool.
3 Beat butter, eggs, sugar and extract in a small bowl with an electric mixer until light and fluffy. Stir in sifted flour and date mixture. Divide mixture into pan holes. Bake about 15 minutes.
4 Meanwhile, make toffee sauce.
5 Serve warm puddings with toffee sauce and a little extra pouring cream, if you like.

toffee sauce Cook sugar in a medium frying pan, over medium heat, without stirring, until sugar melts and turns a dark caramel colour. Gently add the cream (be careful, as it will splatter); stir to combine. Simmer, uncovered, for 1 minute or until sauce thickens slightly.

These cakes should be served straight away. If they are allowed to sit, the gooey centre will firm up and the chocolate won't ooze out when they're cut.

warm chocolate and caramel puddings

125g (4 ounces) butter, softened

⅔ cup (150g) firmly packed brown sugar

2 eggs

½ cup (75g) plain (all-purpose) flour

¼ cup (25g) cocoa powder

1½ tablespoons milk

12 caramel-filled chocolate squares

1 Preheat oven to 200°C/400°F.

2 Grease four 1-cup (250ml) ovenproof dishes; line bases with baking paper.

3 Beat butter and sugar in a small bowl with an electric mixer until light and fluffy. Beat in eggs, one at a time. Stir in sifted flour, cocoa and milk.

4 Divide two-thirds of the mixture into dishes; place three caramel chocolate squares in centre of each dish. Spoon remaining mixture over chocolate squares; smooth surface.

5 Bake about 20 minutes. Stand puddings in dishes for 5 minutes before turning out onto serving plates; serve immediately.

tip The melted chocolate will be hot, so take care when biting into the puddings.

serving suggestion Serve with thick (double) cream or ice-cream, dusted with sifted cocoa powder.

apple and cinnamon crunch cake with cinnamon anglaise

8 small red-skinned apples (800g)

1.5 litres (6 cups) water

2 cups (440g) caster (superfine) sugar

1 cinnamon stick

185g (6 ounces) butter, softened

2 teaspoons vanilla extract

1 cup (220g) caster (superfine) sugar, extra

3 eggs

1 cup (120g) ground almonds

1½ cups (225g) self-raising flour

½ cup (125ml) buttermilk

CINNAMON CRUNCH TOPPING

90g (3 ounces) butter

½ cup firmly packed brown sugar

½ cup plain (all-purpose) flour

3 teaspoons ground cinnamon

CINNAMON ANGLAISE

¾ cup (180ml) pouring cream

1⅓ cups (330ml) milk

1 cinnamon stick

4 egg yolks

¼ cup (55g) caster (superfine) sugar

1 Peel apples, leaving stems intact.
2 Combine the water, sugar and cinnamon in a saucepan large enough to hold apples in a single layer; stir over high heat, without boiling, until sugar dissolves. Bring to the boil, add apples; cover apples with a round of baking paper and a heatproof plate to keep the apples submerged in the syrup. Return to the boil. Reduce heat; simmer, covered, for 8 minutes or until apples are tender. Remove apples from pan with a slotted spoon (be very careful as the syrup will be hot). Cool for 10 minutes.
3 Preheat oven to 160°C/325°F. Grease 26cm (10½-inch) closed springform pan; insert base of pan upside down to make cake easier to remove. Line base with baking paper.
4 Beat butter, extract and extra sugar in a small bowl with an electric mixer until light and fluffy. Beat in eggs, one at a time. Transfer mixture to a large bowl. Stir in ground almonds, sifted flour and buttermilk, in two batches. Spread mixture into pan. Place apples, evenly spaced, around outside edge of pan, pushing apples down to base of pan.
5 Bake 30 minutes.
6 Meanwhile, make cinnamon crunch topping; crumble topping over the cake. Bake for a further 45 minutes. Stand cake in pan 15 minutes.
7 Make cinnamon anglaise; serve with warm cake.

cinnamon crunch topping Melt butter in a small saucepan over medium heat; stir in remaining ingredients. Refrigerate for 15 minutes.

cinnamon anglaise Combine cream, milk and cinnamon in a medium saucepan; bring to the boil. Remove from heat, cover; stand 20 minutes. Whisk egg yolks and sugar in a medium bowl until creamy. Gradually whisk in warm milk mixture. Return mixture to pan; stir over medium-high heat, without boiling, until custard thickens and coats the back of a spoon. Strain into a medium jug; discard cinnamon stick.

chocolate honeycomb
self-saucing pudding

PREP + COOK TIME 40 MINUTES • SERVES 6

*A large pudding will take
about 40 minutes to cook.*

1 cup (150g) self-raising flour

2 tablespoons cocoa powder

½ cup (110g) firmly packed brown sugar

90g (3 ounces) butter, melted

½ cup (125ml) milk

200g (6½ ounces) chocolate-coated honeycomb, chopped finely

1¼ cups (310ml) water

¾ cup (165g) firmly packed brown sugar, extra

2 tablespoons cocoa powder, extra

300ml thickened (heavy) cream

1 Preheat oven to 180°C/350°F. Grease six 1-cup (250ml) individual ovenproof dishes (or a 1.5-litre/ 6-cup ovenproof dish) well.
2 Sift flour, cocoa and sugar into a large bowl. Stir in melted butter, milk and half the honeycomb. Spread mixture into dishes.
3 Boil the water. Sift extra sugar and cocoa evenly over top of puddings; carefully pour boiling water evenly over top of sugar mixture on each pudding. Bake puddings about 30 minutes (or 40 minutes for the large pudding).
4 Meanwhile, beat cream in a small bowl with an electric mixer until soft peaks form.
5 Serve puddings with cream; sprinkle with the remaining chopped honeycomb.

apple sponge puddings

PREP + COOK TIME 40 MINUTES • MAKES 4

4 medium green-skinned apples (600g), peeled, quartered and cored

¼ cup (55g) caster (superfine) sugar

¼ cup (60ml) water

1 cinnamon stick

2 eggs

1 teaspoon vanilla extract

1 tablespoon finely grated lemon rind

¼ cup (55g) caster (superfine) sugar, extra

½ cup (75g) self-raising flour

⅓ cup (25g) shredded coconut

2 teaspoons icing (confectioners') sugar

1 Preheat oven to 180°C/350°F. Grease four 1-cup (250ml) ovenproof dishes.

2 Combine apples, sugar, the water and cinnamon in a medium saucepan; cook, covered, over medium heat, for 8 minutes or until apples are tender. Discard cinnamon. Spoon apple into dishes.

3 Beat eggs, extract, rind and extra sugar in a small bowl with an electric mixer until thick and creamy. Transfer to a medium bowl; fold in sifted flour and coconut. Spoon sponge mixture over apple. Place dishes on oven tray.

4 Bake puddings about 15 minutes or until browned lightly. Stand for 5 minutes before serving dusted with sifted icing sugar; accompany with ice-cream, if you like.

Puddings are best served warm.

Muscat is a sweet dessert wine available from most liquor stores.

honey muscat syrup cake

250g (8 ounces) butter, softened

½ cup (110g) caster (superfine) sugar

½ cup (175g) honey

3 eggs

2 cups (150g) self-raising flour

½ cup (125ml) muscat

½ cup (140g) greek-style yoghurt

ORANGE SYRUP

⅔ cup (160ml) orange juice

½ cup (125ml) water

¾ cup (165g) caster (superfine) sugar

1 tablespoon muscat

YOGHURT TOPPING

2 cups icing (confectioners') sugar

¼ cup greek-style yoghurt

2 tablespoons reserved orange syrup

TO DECORATE

1½ tablespoons freeze dried pomegranate seeds

8 raspberries

1 blood orange, peeled, segmented

1 orange, unpeeled, sliced thinly

1 Preheat oven to 180°C/350°F. Grease a 24cm (9½-inch) bundt pan well (see page 113); sprinkle with a little flour, tap out excess flour.

2 Beat butter and sugar in a small bowl with an electric mixer until light and fluffy. Beat in honey, then eggs, one at a time. Transfer mixture to a large bowl. Stir in sifted flour, muscat and yoghurt in two batches. Spread mixture into pan.

3 Bake about 45 minutes. Turn cake onto a wire rack over a shallow tray.

4 Meanwhile, make orange syrup. Pour hot syrup over hot cake.

5 Make yoghurt topping.

6 Serve cake warm, drizzled with yoghurt topping and topped with fruit.

orange syrup Combine ingredients in a small saucepan; stir over high heat, without boiling, until sugar dissolves. Bring to the boil; remove from heat. Reserve 2 tablespoons syrup for the yoghurt topping.

yoghurt topping Combine sifted icing sugar with the yoghurt and reserved syrup in a small bowl, beat until smooth.

sticky ginger cake with grilled toffee figs

PREP + COOK TIME 1½ HOURS • SERVES 12

250g (8 ounces) butter, softened

1½ cups (330g) caster (superfine) sugar

3 eggs

⅓ cup (115g) golden syrup or treacle

2 cups (300g) plain (all-purpose) flour

1½ teaspoons bicarbonate of soda (baking soda)

2 tablespoons ground ginger

1 tablespoon ground cinnamon

1 large firm pear (330g), peeled, grated coarsely

⅔ cup (160ml) hot water

6 medium fresh figs (360g), halved

1 tablespoon caster (superfine) sugar, extra

TOFFEE SAUCE

1 cup (220g) caster (superfine) sugar

½ cup (125ml) water

300ml thickened (heavy) cream

1 Preheat oven to 180°C/350°F. Grease a deep 22cm (9-inch) square cake pan; line base and sides with baking paper.
2 Beat butter and sugar in a small bowl with an electric mixer until light and fluffy. Beat in eggs, one at a time. Beat in syrup. Transfer mixture to a large bowl; stir in sifted flour, soda and spices, pear and the hot water. Spread mixture into pan.
3 Bake about 1 hour. Stand cake in pan for 10 minutes before turning, top-side up, onto a wire rack.
4 Meanwhile, make toffee sauce.
5 Preheat grill (broiler). Place figs, cut-side up, on an oven tray. Sprinkle extra sugar over cut surface. Grill figs until browned lightly.
6 Top warm cake with figs; serve with warm toffee sauce, and cream or ice-cream, if you like.

toffee sauce Combine sugar and the water in a medium saucepan; stir over high heat, without boiling, until sugar dissolves. Bring to the boil; boil, uncovered, without stirring, until caramel in colour. Remove from heat. Carefully stir in cream (the mixture will spit and bubble). Stir over low heat until toffee pieces are melted and sauce is smooth.

coconut and lemon syrup cake

PREP + COOK TIME 1¼ HOURS • SERVES 8

This cake will keep in an airtight container for up to three days.

125g (4 ounces) butter, softened

1 cup (220g) caster (superfine) sugar

4 eggs

2 cups (160g) desiccated coconut

1 cup (150g) self-raising flour

2 tablespoons desiccated coconut, extra

LEMON SYRUP

1 cup (220g) caster (superfine) sugar

¾ cup (180ml) water

4 x 5cm (2-inch) strips lemon rind

¼ cup (60ml) lemon juice

1 Preheat oven to 160°C/325°F. Grease a deep 20cm (8-inch) round cake pan; line base and side with baking paper.

2 Beat butter and sugar in a small bowl with an electric mixer until light and fluffy. Beat in eggs, one at a time. Transfer mixture to a large bowl; stir in coconut and sifted flour. Spread mixture into pan; sprinkle with extra coconut.

3 Bake about 50 minutes. Cover cake with foil if over-browning.

4 Meanwhile, make lemon syrup.

5 Pour hot lemon syrup over hot cake in pan. Cool.

lemon syrup Stir ingredients in a small saucepan over heat, without boiling, until sugar dissolves; bring to the boil. Reduce heat; simmer, uncovered, without stirring, for 5 minutes. Strain.

nectarine & almond upside-down cake

PREP + COOK TIME 1¼ HOURS • SERVES 9

50g (1½ ounces) butter, chopped

½ cup (110g) firmly packed brown sugar

3 large nectarines (650g), cut into 8 wedges each

125g (4 ounces) butter, extra, softened

1 teaspoon vanilla extract

1¼ cups (275g) caster (superfine) sugar

3 eggs

¾ cup (110g) self-raising flour

¾ cup (110g) plain (all-purpose) flour

¾ cup (180ml) milk

1 cup (120g) ground almonds

⅓ cup (25g) flaked almonds, toasted

1 Preheat oven to 180°C/350°F. Grease 19cm (8-inch) square cake pan; line base and sides with baking paper.

2 Combine chopped butter and brown sugar in a small saucepan, stir over low heat until smooth; pour into base of cake pan. Place nectarine wedges, cut-side down, over caramel mixture.

3 Beat softened butter, extract and caster sugar in a medium bowl with an electric mixer until light and fluffy. Beat in eggs, one at a time. Stir in sifted flours, and milk, in two batches. Stir in ground almonds.

4 Spread mixture into pan; bake about 50 minutes. Stand cake in pan for 15 minutes before turning onto wire rack to cool. Serve sprinkled with flaked almonds; drizzle with any juices left in the cake pan.

Test Kitchen NOTES

Cake is best served warm. Store cake, covered, in the fridge; bring to room temperature before serving.

plum and blueberry crumble cake

200g (6½ ounces) butter, softened

¾ cup (165g) caster (superfine) sugar

2 eggs

1 cup (150g) self-raising flour

1 cup (150g) plain (all-purpose) flour

¾ cup (180ml) milk

1kg (2 pounds) canned whole plums in natural juice, drained

60g (2 ounces) fresh blueberries

2 teaspoons icing (confectioners') sugar

SPICED CRUMBLE TOPPING

½ cup (75g) plain (all-purpose) flour

50g (1½ ounces) cold butter, chopped coarsely

¾ cup (60g) shredded coconut

¼ cup (55g) firmly packed brown sugar

1 teaspoon mixed spice

1 Preheat oven to 180°C/350°F. Grease a deep 22cm (9-inch) closed springform pan; line base and side with baking paper.

2 Make spiced crumble topping.

3 Beat butter and sugar in a medium bowl with an electric mixer until light and fluffy. Beat in eggs, one at a time. Transfer mixture to a large bowl; fold in sifted flours and milk, in two batches. Spread mixture into pan.

4 Halve plums; discard stones. Divide plums and blueberries over cake mixture. Sprinkle crumble topping over fruit.

5 Bake about 1½ hours (cover cake with foil if over-browning). Stand cake in pan for 10 minutes before turning, top-side up, onto a wire rack. Serve cake, warm or at room temperature, dusted with sifted icing sugar.

spiced crumble topping Blend or process ingredients until combined.

serving suggestion Dollop with thick (double) cream.

Test Kitchen
NOTES

This cake will keep in an airtight container, refrigerated, for up to three days. Reheat slices in the microwave to serve warm.

Test Kitchen
NOTES

This cake is best served
warm with cream. Large firm
strawberries can be sliced
lengthways and substituted
for the rhubarb; apple or
nashi can be substituted for
the pear; or a combination of
any of these fruits (including
the rhubarb) can be used.
The cake will keep for one day
in an airtight container in
the refrigerator.

rhubarb and pear custard cake

PREP + COOK TIME 1½ HOURS • SERVES 10

125g (4 ounces) butter, softened

¾ cup (165g) caster (superfine) sugar

2 eggs

1½ cups (225g) self-raising flour

½ cup (60g) ground almonds

2 tablespoons custard powder

½ cup (125ml) milk

3 trimmed stalks rhubarb (250g), cut into 2cm (¾-inch) pieces

1 large pear (330g), peeled, sliced thinly

½ cup (160g) apricot jam

CUSTARD

2 tablespoons custard powder

2 tablespoons caster (superfine) sugar

1 cup (250ml) milk

1 teaspoon vanilla extract

20g (¾ ounce) butter

1 Preheat oven to 180°C/350°F. Grease a deep 22cm (9-inch) round cake pan; line base and side with baking paper.

2 Make custard.

3 Beat butter and sugar in a medium bowl with an electric mixer until light and fluffy; add eggs, one at a time, beating well between additions. Stir in sifted flour, ground almonds, custard powder and milk.

4 Spread half of the cake mixture into pan, top with half the rhubarb and half the pear.

5 Spread cooled custard over fruit; spread remaining cake mixture over custard, top with remaining rhubarb and pear. Bake about 1 hour.

6 Place jam in a small saucepan over low heat; heat jam, stirring, until warmed through. Strain.

7 Stand cake in pan for 5 minutes before turning, top-side up, onto a wire rack; brush top with warm jam. Cool.

custard Combine custard powder and sugar in a small saucepan over medium heat; gradually stir in milk. Stir over heat until mixture boils and thickens. Remove from heat, add extract and butter; stir until butter melts. Cover surface of custard completely with plastic wrap to prevent a skin forming; cool to room temperature (do not refrigerate as mixture will not be spreadable).

4 ways with
COOKIE CUPCAKES

OREO

Crush 3 small individual packets of mini Oreo biscuits.
Combine crushed biscuits with butter cream in a
small bowl. Half-fill piping bag with butter cream.
Pipe swirls of butter cream on top of each cupcake;
top with a mini Oreo.

CHOC-CHIP COOKIE

Crush 75g (2½ ounces) choc-chip biscuits. Combine
with butter cream in a small bowl. Half-fill piping
bag with butter cream. Pipe swirls of butter cream
on top of each cupcake. Coarsely break six more
biscuits into large pieces. Top butter cream with
biscuit pieces; sprinkle with dark chocolate bits.

Test Kitchen NOTES

You need 12 chocolate cupcakes for each recipe (see chocolate heart cake recipe, page 50) and 1 quantity butter cream (page 115). You also need a large piping bag fitted with a 2cm (¾-inch) plain piping tube.

M&M COOKIE DOUGH

Preheat oven to 180°C/350°F. Beat 175g (5½ ounces) softened M&M cookie dough into butter cream in a small bowl with an electric mixer; fold through 2 tablespoons mini M&M's. Cut remaining cookie dough into 2cm (¾-inch) rounds (you will need 12 rounds). Place rounds on an oven tray; bake for 8 minutes. Cool cookies on tray. Half-fill piping bag with butter cream; pipe swirls on top of cupcakes; top with cookies and sprinkle with extra mini M&M's.

100s & 1000s

Crush 12 biscuits from 2 packets of mini hundreds & thousands biscuits. Half-fill piping bag with butter cream. Pipe swirls of butter cream on top of each cupcake. Top with crushed biscuits, and sprinkle with 100's & 1000's, if you like.

vanilla pear almond cake

8 corella pears (800g)

2½ cups (625ml) water

1 strip lemon rind

1¾ cups (385g) caster (superfine) sugar

1 vanilla bean, halved lengthways

125g (4 ounces) butter, softened

3 eggs

⅔ cup (160g) sour cream

⅔ cup (100g) plain (all-purpose) flour

⅔ cup (100g) self-raising flour

40g (1½ ounces) dark (semi-sweet) chocolate, chopped coarsely

¼ cup (40g) blanched almonds, roasted, chopped coarsely

½ cup (60g) ground almonds

Cake is best made on day of serving.

1 Peel pears, leaving stems intact.

2 Combine the water, rind and 1 cup of the sugar in a medium saucepan. Scrape vanilla bean seeds into saucepan, then add pod. Stir over high heat, without boiling, until sugar dissolves. Add pears; bring to the boil. Reduce heat; simmer, covered, for 30 minutes or until pears are just tender.

3 Transfer pears to a medium bowl; bring syrup to the boil. Boil, uncovered, until syrup reduces by half. Using tongs, remove pod. Cool syrup completely.

4 Preheat oven to 200°C/400°F. Insert base of a 23cm (9-inch) springform pan upside down in pan to give a flat base; grease pan.

5 Beat butter and remaining sugar in a medium bowl with an electric mixer until light and fluffy. Beat in eggs, one at a time. Add sour cream; beat until just combined. Stir in 2 tablespoons of the syrup, then combined sifted flours, nuts, chocolate and almonds.

6 Spread mixture into pan. Cut pears in halves or quarters; gently push pears into batter, pushing to the bottom of the pan. Bake for 1½ hours or until a skewer inserted into the centre comes out clean. Stand cake in pan for 10 minutes before turning, top-side up, onto a wire rack.

7 Serve cake warm, brushed with remaining syrup.

serving suggestion Serve warm with vanilla bean ice-cream or custard.

Cooking TECHNIQUES

Sponge roll (a)

Turn the sponge onto a piece of sugared baking paper. Carefully peel lining paper from sponge using a long spatula; the spatula's pressure will prevent the base of the sponge from lifting and tearing.

Sponge roll (b)

Using the baking paper as a guide, roll the warm sponge loosely from one side (the recipe will indicate to roll it from the long or short side). Unroll, then cool. Spread with jam, then reroll from the same side.

Level a cake top

Many cakes need to have their domed tops cut off so the cakes sit flat on a cake board or plate. Use a serrated knife to cut the cake; place your other hand on top of the cake to stop it moving.

Melting chocolate

Place broken chocolate in a heatproof bowl over a pan of simmering water; the water mustn't touch the base of the bowl. Stir chocolate until smooth, then remove from the pan as soon as it's melted.

Small chocolate curls

Have a large, unbroken bar of chocolate at room temperature. Drag a vegetable peeler down the length of the chocolate along the side to make small curls.

Large chocolate curls

To make large curls, place the chocolate block, flat-side up, on a board. Drag a cheese slicer over the block; the harder you press, the thicker the curls.

Cut a cake into layers (a)

Use bamboo skewers as a guide for the knife to split the cake into layers. If the cake is large, long skewers can be pushed through the cake, from one side to the other.

Cut a cake into layers (b)

If the cake is small, use toothpicks to mark the layer. Using a serrated knife, cut the cake just above the skewers, you should feel the knife touch the skewers as you cut through the cake.

Covering a cake

Cover the cake side only with frosting. Spread whatever covering is to be used in a large pan and, holding the cake like a wheel, roll the side of the cake until covered. The top can be now be covered.

Bundt or baba pans

Use a pastry brush to thickly grease the pan with melted (or softened) butter. Place the pan in the freezer for a few minutes, then sprinkle with a little flour; turn the pan upside down and tap out excess flour.

Beating egg whites

Beat egg whites in a clean, dry bowl increasing speed as the egg whites thicken, until soft foamy peaks form. Start adding the sugar at this stage.

Angel food cakes

To unmould an angel food cake, turn the pan upside down onto the bench over baking paper. Do not move or shake the pan; the cake will fall out under its own weight while cooling.

Tips for BAKING CAKES

The first time you use a recipe when baking, read it all the way through so you know what the steps are, what equipment you need, and if there is any additional standing, refrigerating or freezing time, or if you need to start the recipe the day before. Then, when you make the recipe, make notes next to it – these notes are a good reference to have the next time you bake.

TESTING THE CAKE IS DONE

The baking times given in our recipes should only be used as a guide; there are too many factors beyond our control to give absolutely accurate baking times in any recipe. Believe it or not, the weather can have an impact on baking, as will the oven (as every oven bakes differently). As you get towards the end of the baking time, open the oven door and quickly have a look at the cake; if it's clearly nowhere near done, close the door, re-set the timer to a new checking time (another 5-10 minutes, depending on how underdone it is).

If you think the cake might be done, then touch the top of the cake with your fingers, gently but firmly enough to 'feel' it. You should feel a crust and a firmness, and the cake should look like it might be wanting to pull away slightly from the side/s of the pan. Also, when a skewer is inserted into the centre of the cake, it will come out clean.

BUTTER CAKES

Most butter cakes respond well to being tested with a fine metal skewer, do this while the cake is still in the oven, but with the rack slightly pulled out. Gently push the skewer through the thickest part of the cake, avoiding cracks, to the bottom of the pan. Gently withdraw the skewer, if you see cake mixture on the skewer, continue to bake a little longer. If you don't see cake mixture, run your thumb and finger down the skewer and feel for any wet cake mixture. The skewer should come out of a cooked cake looking and feeling shiny and clean.

MUD CAKES & BROWNIES

It can be tricky to get these to just the right texture. They are usually made by a 'melt and mix' method, and the recipes are always high in fat and sugar, so they often develop a sugary crust that can make testing difficult. Use a skewer for testing, as you would for a butter cake. Sometimes the crust will 'wipe' away any sign of uncooked mixture on the skewer, try sliding the skewer under the crust to get a better idea of what the mixture is really like – if it's cooked or not. Make a note of the time and temperature you use, so that you can turn them out with the texture you like best every time.

ANGEL FOOD & CHIFFON CAKES

These cakes are American in origin and are an incredibly light type of sponge cake; they both rely on lots of carefully beaten egg whites for aeration. It's important to not grease the tube pans in which they're cooked, as the light airy mixture needs to cling to the side of the pan as it rises in the oven. To test if an angel food or chiffon cake is cooked, check it just before the cooking time is up. Lightly touch the surface of the cake, as you would for a sponge cake. The cake pans have 'feet', so that the pan can be turned upside down onto a baking-paper lined bench; the cake is suspended as it cools. Once the cake reaches room temperature, it will usually drop out of the pan by itself, if it doesn't, gently ease the cake away from the side of the pan with a metal spatula.

SPONGE CAKES

Don't test a sponge cake with a skewer or it will deflate. Towards the end of the baking time, open the oven gently and have a look, it should be well-risen, browned and not shrunken from the side of the pan.

Gently feel the top of the sponge with your fingers, if it feels slightly firm, gently press your fingers onto the crust, your fingers shouldn't leave an imprint. Have a wire rack ready, covered with baking paper. Gently shake the pan to make sure the sponge is free from the base and side of the pan, then turn the sponge, top-side up, onto the wire rack.

Never leave a sponge to cool in the pan, as the heat from the pan will continue to cook the sponge, which will cause it to shrink and become dry.

LOAVES & BREADS

These are usually baked in narrow pans, such as bar, ring, loaf or nut roll tins; they rise quickly and quite a lot. As a result, most loaf- and ring-shaped cakes crack along the centre. Test loaves and breads with a skewer, as you would a butter cake.

CUPCAKES, MUFFINS & FRIANDS

These all cook quite quickly because of their size, so it's important not to overcook them. You can usually tell if they're cooked by simply looking at, and touching, them. If in doubt, use a skewer, as test as you would for a butter cake.

Icing RECIPES

Butter cream

Basic butter cream is also known as vienna cream; the flavour can be varied by adding any extract or essence you like.

125g (4 ounces) unsalted butter, softened

1½ cups (240g) icing sugar (confectioners' sugar)

2 tablespoons milk

Beat the butter in a small bowl with an electric mixer until as white as possible. Gradually beat in half the sifted icing sugar, milk, then the remaining icing sugar.

Chocolate variation: Sift ⅓ cup (35g) cocoa powder in with the first batch of icing sugar.

White Chocolate Ganache

360g (11½ ounces) white chocolate

½ cup (125ml) pouring cream

1 Break the chocolate into a food processor; process until chocolate is finely chopped.
2 Bring cream to the boil in a small saucepan; remove from heat.
3 Add chocolate to cream; stir until ganache is smooth.
4 Cool mixture to room temperature before beating or whipping ganache to the desired consistency.

Ganache

Ganache is a mixture of melted chocolate and cream. It is wonderfully simple to make and versatile to use. It can be used while it's still warm as a glaze over a cake. Or, let the ganache partly set, either at a cool room temperature or in the refrigerator, then beat it with a wooden spoon until it's spreadable – making it a perfect filling or frosting for cakes.

Whipping ganache: Ganache can be refrigerated for around 30 minutes, or until it becomes thick and spreadable, then whipped with an electric mixer until it increases in volume and becomes fluffy. Ganache will keep in the refrigerator, covered tightly, for about two weeks (stand at room temperature to soften before use), or frozen for 3 months; thaw overnight in the refrigerator, or thaw it in the microwave oven using short bursts of low power.

Dark or Milk Chocolate Ganache

200g (6½ ounces) milk or dark chocolate, broken into pieces

½ cup (125ml) pouring cream

1 Bring the cream to the boil in a small saucepan; remove from heat.
2 Break chocolate into pan with the hot cream; stir until smooth.
3 Cool mixture to room temperature before beating or whipping ganache to the desired consistency.

Colouring butter cream: Use a skewer to dab a tiny amount of colouring onto the butter cream. Mix the colouring through thoroughly before adding any more.

Whipping ganache: Cool ganache in the fridge for around 30 minutes, stirring occasionally. Beat the ganache with an electric mixer until light and fluffy.

GLOSSARY

ALMONDS

flaked paper thin almond slices.

ground also called almond meal.

vienna toffee-coated almonds.

BAKING POWDER a raising agent; consists of two parts cream of tartar to one part bicarbonate of soda.

BICARBONATE OF SODA also known as baking soda.

BUTTER 125g butter is equal to 1 stick (4 ounces).

BUTTERMILK originally the term given to the slightly sour liquid left after butter was churned from cream, today it is made similarly to yoghurt. Sold alongside fresh milk products in supermarkets. Despite its name, buttermilk is low in fat.

CHOCOLATE

dark (semi-sweet) made of cocoa liquor, cocoa butter and a little added sugar.

milk most popular eating chocolate, mild and very sweet; similar in makeup to dark chocolate with the difference being the addition of milk solids.

white contains no cocoa solids but derives its sweet flavour from cocoa butter. Very sensitive to heat.

CINNAMON available in pieces (sticks or quills) and in ground form.

COCOA POWDER also known as unsweetened cocoa.

dutch-processed is treated with an alkali to neutralize its acids. It has a reddish-brown colour, a mild flavour, and is easy to dissolve in liquids.

COCONUT

desiccated concentrated, unsweetened, dried and finely shredded coconut flesh.

shredded unsweetened thin strips of dried coconut flesh.

CORNFLOUR (CORNSTARCH) used as a thickening agent in cooking. Wheaten cornflour is made from wheat rather than corn and gives sponge cakes a lighter texture (due to the fact wheaten cornflour has some gluten).

CREAM we use fresh cream, also known as pouring, single and pure cream, unless otherwise stated. It has no additives unlike commercially thickened cream. Minimum fat content 35%.

sour cream a thick cultured soured cream. Minimum fat content 35%.

thickened a whipping cream that contains a thickener. Has a minimum fat content of 35%.

CREAM OF TARTAR the acid ingredient in baking powder.

CUSTARD POWDER instant mixture used to make pouring custard; similar to North American instant pudding mixes.

EARL GREY, FRENCH earl grey blended with flower (rose) petals and slivers of fruit (citrus). Available from specialist tea shops. Earl Grey tea is fine to use.

FLOUR

plain also called all-purpose flour.

self-raising plain or wholemeal flour with baking powder; make at home in the proportion of 1 cup plain flour to 2 teaspoons baking powder.

GELATINE a thickening agent. We use powdered gelatine; is also available in sheets known as leaf gelatine.

GINGER

glacé fresh ginger root preserved in sugar syrup; crystallised ginger can be substituted if rinsed with warm water and dried well before use.

ground also called powdered ginger; cannot be substituted for fresh ginger.

GOLDEN SYRUP a by-product of refined sugar cane; pure maple syrup or honey can be substituted.

HAZELNUT also called filbert; plump, grape-sized, rich, sweet nut with a brown inedible skin that is removed by rubbing heated nuts together vigorously in a clean tea towel.

ground also called hazelnut meal.

MARSALA a fortified Italian wine produced in the region surrounding the Sicilian city of Marsala; it has an intense amber colour and complex aroma, and is often used in cooking.

MAPLE SYRUP a thin syrup distilled from the sap of the maple tree. Maple-flavoured syrup or pancake syrup is not an adequate substitute for the real thing.

MASCARPONE a fresh cultured-cream product made similarly to yogurt. Whiteish to creamy yellow in colour, with a buttery-rich texture; it is soft and creamy.

MIXED SPICE a classic spice mixture generally containing caraway, allspice, coriander, cumin, nutmeg and ginger.

ORANGE BLOSSOM WATER this concentrated flavouring is made from orange blossoms.

PERSIAN FAIRY FLOSS also sold as pashmak, is a form of fairy floss made from sesame and sugar. It has a different texture and its strands are said to resemble sheep's wool (pashmak in Persian means little wool). It is available from specialist food stores, some delicatessens and cake decorating suppliers.

POMEGRANATE dark-red, leathery-skinned fruit about the size of an orange. Filled with hundreds of seeds wrapped in an edible lucent-crimson pulp that have a unique tangy sweet-sour flavour.

RHUBARB a plant with long, green-red stalks (the only edible part of the plant); it becomes sweet and edible when cooked.

ROSEWATER made from rose petals.

SUGAR

brown a very soft, finely granulated sugar retaining molasses for its characteristic colour and flavour.

caster also known as superfine or finely granulated table sugar. The fine crystals dissolve easily so it is perfect for cakes, meringues and desserts.

icing also called confectioners' sugar or powdered sugar; pulverised granulated sugar crushed with a small amount of cornflour added.

pure icing also called confectioners' or powdered sugar; has no added cornflour.

white coarsely granulated table sugar, also known as crystal sugar.

SUMAC a purple-red, astringent spice ground from berries growing on shrubs flourishing wild around the Mediterranean; adds a tart, lemony flavour to foods.

TREACLE thick, dark syrup not unlike molasses; a by-product of sugar refining.

VANILLA

bean dried long, thin pod from a tropical golden orchid; the tiny black seeds impart a sweet vanilla flavour.

extract vanilla beans that have been submerged in alcohol. Vanilla essence is not a suitable substitute.

INDEX

This book is published in 2015 by Octopus Publishing Group Limited
based on materials licensed to it by Bauer Media Books, Australia
Bauer Media Books is a division of Bauer Media Pty Limited.
54 Park St, Sydney; GPO Box 4088, Sydney, NSW 2001, Australia
phone (+61) 2 9282 8618; fax (+61) 2 9126 3702
www.awwcookbooks.com.au

MEDIA GROUP

BAUER MEDIA BOOKS

Publisher – Jo Runciman
Editorial & food director – Pamela Clark
Director of sales, marketing & rights – Brian Cearnes
Creative director – Hieu Chi Nguyen
Art director & designer – Hannah Blackmore
Senior editor – Wendy Bryant
Food editor – Emma Braz

Published and Distributed in the United Kingdom by Octopus Publishing Group
Endeavour House
189 Shaftesbury Avenue
London WC2H 8JY
phone (+44) (0) 207 632 5400; fax (+44) (0) 207 632 5405
info@octopus-publishing.co.uk;
www.octopusbooks.co.uk

Printed by Toppan Printing Co, Hong Kong

International foreign language rights, Brian Cearnes, Bauer Media Books bcearnes@bauer-media.com.au

A catalogue record for this book is available from the British Library.
ISBN: 978 1909770 21 8 (paperback)

© Bauer Media Pty Ltd 2015
ABN 18 053 273 546

ALSO FROM THE BEST-SELLING COOKERY SERIES OF ALL TIME

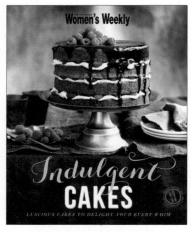

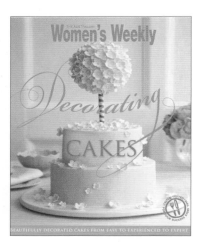

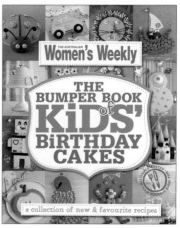

To order books visit www.octopusbooks.co.uk or telephone +44 (0)1903 828 503